After-Images
W. D. Snodgrass

AFTER-IMAGES:

AUTOBIOGRAPHICAL SKETCHES

W. D. Snodgrass

BOA Editions, Ltd. ❧ Rochester, NY ❧ 1999

LC #: 98–076204
ISBN: 1–880238–75–6 cloth
ISBN: 1–880238–76–4 paper

First Edition
99 00 01 02 7 6 5 4 3 2 1

Publications by BOA Editions, Ltd.—
a not-for-profit corporation under section 501 (c) (3)
of the United States Internal Revenue Code—
are made possible with the assistance of grants from
the Literature Program of the New York State Council on the Arts,
the Literature Program of the National Endowment for the Arts,
the Lannan Foundation, the Sonia Raiziss Giop Charitable Foundation,
as well as from the Mary S. Mulligan Charitable Trust,
the County of Monroe, NY,
and from many individual supporters, including
Richard Garth & Mimi Hwang, Judy & Dane Gordon, Robert & Willy Hursh,
and Pat & Michael Wilder.

Cover Design: Daphne Poulin-Stofer
Cover Art: "The Locked House" by DeLoss McGraw,
courtesy of the artist
Typesetting: Richard Foerster
Printed in the United States by McNaughton & Gunn
BOA Logo: Mirko

BOA Editions, Ltd.
Richard Garth, Chair
A. Poulin, Jr., President & Founder (1976–1996)
260 East Avenue
Rochester, NY 14604

www.boaeditions.org

Forget not the unforgettable.
        —Koz'ma Prutkov

For Kathy
Keep on and you get it right!

PREFACE

I hope it will be clear that this book consists of sketches conceived separately and at widely separated intervals; it certainly does not intend the complete view of my life which an autobiography would. Though I have tried to coax these images into appearing a little more comfortably together, I have chiefly been concerned with the shape and unity of the individual pieces. The last several sketches happen to end near the present time, but each moves in its own separate time span; the book is organized by subject, not chronology.

I have been called a "confessional" poet, a term I heartily dislike. I am in no sense religious, and I have no interest in the lurid revelations of afternoon TV shows or of "true confessions" publications. I believe that no subject matter should be barred from poetry, but that those matters usually considered personal or private should not be broached for their own sensational sake, where they could damage people still living, or might lead to self-display or self-justification. Autobiographical details, if they appear, should satisfy the poem's needs, not the author's hankering for notice or admiration.

I think the same is true in prose. These essays review matters which I hope will be of interest, over which I have some authority, and which I can evoke without harming anyone's reputation more than my own.

—W. D. Snodgrass

CONTENTS

I. GOOD HOUSEKEEPING

When I was eight or ten, one outsider still visited our house—Uncle Stew, my father's younger brother, who came to play chess. Earlier, my father had given blindfolded and/or simultaneous chess exhibitions; once he almost got a draw from Sammy Reshevsky, the world's champion. I seem to recall rumors that others had once come to play with him, but by that time there was only Stew—good-natured, lackadaisical, and comic. Soon, though, he too said or did something my mother could find offensive; he, too, was banished. Or, rather, the house was made unbearable to him.

After that, there was only an occasional maid or cleaning woman. Against each arose a growing battery of complaints which eventually led to dismissal, though these complaints merely disguised the real problem. Each in turn had committed the same transgression: actually cleaning the house, moving things, creating a recognizable order, or, worst of all, throwing out some part of that incredible mare's nest and so rousing my mother's smoldering rage and resentment. It was as if they did such things intending to shame her or to belie the reasons she gave for her martyrdom to endless drudgery.

Only one maid, Elsie, diverged from this pattern. Perhaps she merely felt she must escape; but we were still in the Depression—she did not dare quit. In our bathroom, she washed out her own underpants and draped them, their stitched crotch so visible as to seem fluorescent, on my father's washcloth rack. Perhaps he did not pick them up, did not actually wash his face with them. But he did indeed become indignant (or realized he had better seem indignant) and uttered a classic American phrase: That girl must go! Go she did and to our dismay began to spread reports about conditions in our house, especially the food: everything came out of cans! I wonder if I began to suspect then that something was profoundly wrong. Much later I realized that many welfare families in that small industrial city ate better than we did. In any case, Elsie too passed into the world of outer dark—or, as I came to see it, of outer light.

A terrible darkness had, indeed, settled through our house. Perhaps I should say houses, though the trouble did not really focus until, after various rentals, we finally bought one when I was in my middle teens. It was a fine, big, orange brick house in Beaver Falls, Pennsylvania, sitting high on a large corner lot a block from Geneva College. Very experimental when it was built in the 1920s, it had rounded corners whose curved windows would raise only six or eight inches, but swung on a central pivot. The first summer, those windows stood wide; light and air poured through the filmy curtains, filling the immense living room and flowing around the comfortably scattered furniture.

A large central hall fronted the wide stairway with its squared oak newel posts and oak paneling. On each side were the huge living and dining rooms, high-ceilinged, each with a tiled fireplace flanked by glassed-in bookcases; the paneling and moldings here were a local, already extinct cherry. In the cellar had been a central cleaning system but that was already gone when we moved in: we came to mourn its loss as others might an exiled prince.

How solid that house had seemed—a friend said it looked like an old soldier's home in the middle of a football field!—and how frail it proved before my mother's onslaught. The rooms began to take in more and more unnecessary, progressively more dilapidated furniture. She painted the hallways the color of clotted blood, blocked off the windows with closed Venetian blinds and heavy drapes; in time, air conditioners were installed. Next, she stained the woodwork and the patterned oak floors a dark, excremental brown, painted the tilework around the fireplaces black. Then she began to cram every cranny of that once bright and spacious dwelling with things, things, things.

She bought trinkets by the thousands: black china panthers, potmetal swordsmen and chevaliers, ceramic milkmaids and imitation Hummel children, decorated plates. On the walls, dozens of trivets jostled against paintings, mirrors, simulated tapestries of every period and style. Though we came to have a fair amount of money (much later my brother told me, to my utter astonishment, that for a while my father had been a millionaire), she never purchased one good object, be it plate, glass, tablecloth, or vase. She bought instead six cheap ones, certain to break, then scrupulously saved all the pieces (albeit irretrievably scattered into different drawers, boxes, bowls all over the house), promising to repair them when she got time. Of course, she never got time; time was like space—to be driven out at any cost. We kept a sort of dusty museum where the fragments of Osiris might be carefully preserved but where the springtime would never arrive for their reassembly.

Quiet, being a form of order, also had to go. Eventually there were two television sets, besides the several radios, belaboring the air from different rooms at once. Someone was invariably practicing. My sister Barbara played the piano; Shirley, the saxophone and cello; I played both violin and piano, then later—I am not making this up—tympani. That I practiced on the third floor cannot have been a significant mercy. After I moved away, that place was taken by my younger brother with his trap drums and ear-shattering records. Discarded cymbals from his set hung in the big double doorways (their sliding panels long since jammed) together with strings of bells—Indian elephant bells, South American llama bells, cow bells, children's bells, school bells, strings of finger cymbals, ankle bells—all dangling on long, contiguous, mismatched cords. One's passage from room to room was necessarily accompanied by a sort of atonal gamelan orchestra; sitting still became worthwhile. Meantime, though, the dogs and cats chased about, abetting the hurly-burly and confusion.

My mother had had a fine classical education, nine years of Latin, three of Greek; she had taught classics and coached basketball. Now she ordered six or eight times as many ladies' magazines as she could read. These, together with *Life, Saturday Evening Post, Colliers*, church bulletins, DAR pamphlets and innumerable mail-order catalogs, piled up behind both living-room couches till the piles drew level with their backs. Every vacancy was filled: chests, closets, drawers, cabinets, bookcases. Books overflowed into the corners and began to line the hallways. Everywhere were broken toys, broken appliances and tools, broken furniture, broken china or ceramic animals. The basement filled up with all this, not to mention years of old newspapers and magazines. The sewers backed up occasionally, soaking these papers; the stench grew. Termites, breeding there, soon branched out into the main wooden structures of the house. In places, you could stick your thumb through the door frames like papier-mâché.

Of course, it could never have been easy to clean house there. Iron and steel works surrounded our city, Beaver Falls; walking the dog at night, you were horizoned by the distant clang and clatter of mills and foundries. We never heard this, though, unless there was a strike and it stopped. One learns ignorance of many things; we took in factory sounds, the reek and smoke of industry, with the air we breathed. No one really expected the mills to screen their chimneys as ordered; they, after all, were the *real* government. In a few years, your lungs turned permanently from pink to gray. Perhaps my mother was still trying to clean when I was quite young—I remember her dusting and washing the windows; within two hours, balls of greasy soot and grit, like peppercorns, had settled on the sills.

Years later, when I lived near Syracuse but was briefly away, water got into our basement and the oil furnace blew up. When I came back into that house, exhausted by hours of driving, I thought my eyes were failing; everything had gone dim. Then I picked up a rubber band only to see its brilliant outline, sharp and shining white, on the paper lying under it—like a fossil or the mouth of a tunnel you could still see behind you. Beaver Falls was like that. The wallpaper, freshly washed clothes, papers in desk drawers, keepsakes shut in chests or closets—everything went gray. Sometimes even yet, I will find, in one of my father's books, a strip of paper with a sharply defined black tip that had once protruded from the pages to mark his place. How swiftly those little banners and guideposts faded into the general slatey gray.

According to *A Hole Is to Dig*, a marvelous book of children's definitions, floors are so you don't see the hole your house is built on. According to my brother, our house was built upon not one but *four* basements: the first, filled to the ceiling with broken toys; the second, with used kitty litter; the third, with old, crumpled money; the last basement down (like a department store, or Dante's introverted depths), used Band-Aids. A literary friend to whom I had once described the house paraphrased Keats to say that we had loaded every rift with ordure. To say the house was full of crap would now seem a silly euphemism; then, it would have been a fatal impropriety: the truth. One could find cat or dog shit on every floor, not to mention (as, of course, one dared not) the garbage, the spoilage, the trash, the leavings and broken odd ends. All these grew precious to my mother: "We had so little when I was young," she said. As her resentment against the world, against all other living beings, deepened and festered, all this came to seem a sort of force, a dark and incalculable power collected inside her fortress (she later added a stockade fence) against all that wickedness she felt gathering outside.

Gradually, light fixtures got broken, lost their bulbs, ceased to work; everyone was driven by an almost palpable gloom down to the dining room where she worked under the chandelier and a standing bridge lamp. In time, it became impossible to work, read, or even sit anywhere else in the house. One might be pardoned for drifting into the living room to watch the TV or pausing to watch the different program in the kitchen; it was strictly understood one must then gravitate back to the dining room, the center of light and energy for that obscurely driven establishment.

One of my wives said she had had a cousin whose mother was such a bad cook that he was thirty-five before he discovered you could make toast without scraping it. It seems to me that until I was drafted at eighteen, I did not really believe in fresh vegetables. The few that had entered our house were thought to be inedible and measures were taken to see that they conformed to this opinion.

Twice a week my mother went to the grocery and brought home great piles of foodstuffs and supplies—three times what we needed. Still in their bulky, brown paper sacks, these were at once deposited in every clearable space in the kitchen; there, such already was the chaos that they seemed to disappear as if dropped overboard in mid-ocean. After three or four days she would get back to recover the sacks and start separating what had spoiled, storing the remains in the refrigerator—to continue, more slowly, spoiling.

On Sundays, we *did* get a few of the less wilted lettuce leaves or a tomato slathered with salt, sugar, and mayonnaise to cover any remaining, or unfortunately ripening, flavor. They became a salad that accompanied our boiled beef, mashed potatoes, and canned peas or string beans. This was followed by the one delicious thing my mother made—a cherry or apple pie. This Sunday meal never varied; neither did our weekday menu: the leftovers from Sunday, an occasional hamburger, canned soups, canned hash, canned stew. The canned vegetables were, like the Sunday beef—and the weekday hamburgers!—boiled in water. I have encountered few more revolting sights than that large black skillet half filled with greasy water and large fecal wads of boiling hamburger. There they stayed until safely freed of all flavor, texture, or nutritional value. That was poured onto the pets' food or down the drain. We may have had the healthiest sewer pipes in western Pennsylvania.

Her masterpiece was frozen orange juice. It must have taken years of careful experiment to render it not merely flavorless, as at best it is, but actually disgusting. I shall allow the secret of her method to pass into oblivion; it took twice as long as the normal method and few would find the time and patience in these days of fast foods and flash cookery.

The pets fared better. We began with a series of Pekingese; pampered and ill-tempered, they acted out against others those uglier drives which, in my mother, were repressed into silence and an air of righteous martyrdom. In time, these pedigreed ogres gave way to a nondescript collection of mongrels and stray cats—which still received the Pekes' special care. One evening, between chess games, Uncle Stew wandered into the kitchen, hunting as usual for a snack. When my mother came downstairs, he complimented her on her delicious hash. She protested that she'd made none; he insisted he had just eaten it and had found it good. He had wolfed down the goulash of meat and vegetables she always cooked for the animals. He may have known they ate better than we did; still, the idea turned him quite literally green. In time, she had two dogs and two cats. When someone remarked that this matched her two boys and two girls, she said (of the pets), "But *they* don't talk back." Neither did we, though furtive thoughts may have shown through.

Our kitchen looked like, and was, a disaster center. Every space on its walls was covered with pans, pots, kettles; they, in turn, were covered with heavy sweaters of grease, dust, and industrial grit. Later, there were two ovens, neither fully operational due, at least partly, to layers of baked-on, burned-on grease. Almost every day she had a fire on one of these stoves; always prepared, she kept a large bin of salt at hand, from which she scooped great handfuls onto the fire, reassuring anyone nearby that there was nothing to worry about. Centered in the room, blocking access to everything else, stood a large mangle which, for many years, had not worked. Every flat surface was covered with piles and piles of dirty clothes, clean clothes (unless you wanted some), dirty plates, lost shoes, broken tools, jars of peanut butter, small containers of paper clips, beads, broken barrettes, marbles, rubber bands, stale sandwich cookies, gray potato chips, brittle sticks of erstwhile chewing gum.

Once a week my mother got down and scrubbed the kitchen floor—maneuvering, somehow, around the feet of all the appliances, step stools, bowls of pet food, cat pans. Once convinced all was clean and proper, she put down newspapers over the whole area. These stayed until the following week when she scrubbed again. As they were trampled over, kicked about, tattered, the place grew tangled as a forest floor. In among the papers, out of sight, were four or five pans of dog food, cat food, dog water, cat water, partially contained in former cooking pots which, like their besweatered cousins on the walls, had round bottoms from having often burned dry. Some had handles; some, metal rods which had once supported handles; some, holes where rods for handles had previously been. You could not pass that way without kicking over at least one, filling the darkened areas under the papers with spoiled pet food, or your own socks and shoes with oozy water.

Once, when I was ten or so, Stew took me on a drive to visit a customer. Coming back, we stopped at a restaurant and had spaghetti; I had never imagined so much flavor. Yet when asked about it later, I complained about its dryness—and was reproached for ingratitude to our relative. After further experience, as a rebellious teenager, I dared report that spaghetti was *good*. When my mother discovered you could get it in a can, get it without flavor, spaghetti was finally admitted into the canon of edibility. But at that earlier time, I think I knew a scolding for ingratitude was nothing compared to the penalty for liking anything we did not eat at home.

So strong was the injunction to praise our mother's cooking that, like bungling politicians, we came to believe our own lies. I once made the error of asking home to lunch a young woman who'd caught my fancy, together with another young couple. (This woman, Lila Hank, despite what should have been sufficient warning, became my first wife.) Here was folly compounded; my mother had suggested I invite them, but little dreamed I might actually disobey that first law of our decalogue: Thou shalt bring no outside observers into Thy Mother's House. I still recall my friends' looks of helpless distress and disgust as they choked down their bowls of grease-covered sludge. It was not especially worse than usual; I must have begun to notice something by that time.

Much earlier, when I was three or four, a neighbor took me to visit a farm family who served us some apple pie with cheese. It was that taste, plain American farm cheese, that, fifteen years later in a U.S. Navy mess hall, I suddenly recognized (as Proust his madeleine dipped in exotic flavor)—a taste not openly forbidden, merely missing from our world and necessarily evil: Mother did not eat it.

What my mother *did* eat was another matter. At first, I think, she ate much of what she fed us. In time, growing wiser, she became allergic to most of our fare—especially after she had acceded to some of our requests for flavor. As we grew older, I seldom saw her eat anything but cottage cheese—plain cottage cheese with sugar on it; such variants as pimiento or pineapple would have upset her stomach. Still, one could not be sure. She slept only a few hours in the middle of the night; whether she ate more then, while we slept, one cannot know.

Of course, my mother's way with food matched her methods throughout the house. The cost of driving out so much—time, space, and all forms of order—grew very high, indeed. When only my father, mother, and brother were left at home alone—in the late 1940s or early '50s—she had $1,000 housekeeping money every month. This seldom covered the bills and taxes it was supposed to pay. I asked my father where in the world it all went—I was then supporting a wife and child on $3,200 a year. He looked at me with genuine wonderment and said, "Do you know, I've sometimes thought she must be keeping a man!" But you'd have had to know my mother to appreciate the giddy hilarity of that.

In the midst of that still unimaginable clatter and clutter, our insane jumble and confusion, my father every evening (if he was home from his office) would wash his hands, unfold a card table in the dining room and start to work. He had a den with a large handsome desk, but, under pretext of helping him as an extra typist on some job, my mother had rendered that room nearly impenetrable. First, he laid out his office: lead pencils, dark red or green Bakelite and minutely adjustable, like a row of precision instruments on a surgeon's tray, set up his pile of post-bound ledgers on one side, then spread out the huge, yellow balance sheets he was auditing for some business or industrial enterprise. Slowly and meticulously, he began to enter the exacting lines and columns of figures which would reveal the structure and course of operations, the outlays and income, the financial health or illness of that concern. Balancing those neat rows of figures would also support our family and its whole hodgepodge of squalor and wreckage. Even then, he had no books on his own household and no least notion where his money was vanishing.

❦

II. PARALYSIS

Christian Morgenstern, the German comic poet, wrote many
verses about a fantastic inventor named Korf:

THE INDOOR AIR

Korf invents an indoor air
So thick and corpulent whatever
Gets into it stays stuck there.

Somewhat midway like the feather
Quill with which he wrote no more
When the maidservant bipped his door—

In brief, gives it an alibi
Up in mid-air, an elsewhere whether
Here or there, never mind how or where.

—Translated with Lore Segal

If he'd had a patent, Korf could have sued my family for a small
fortune. Clearly, no new air would come into our house; the big
pivoting windows were clamped and puttied shut. A stench of
sewers and rotting papers welled up from the basement, kitty litter
filled the coal bin, animal excrement all through the house added its
special piquancy. The air, moreover, was heavy with dust, with the
soot and reek of factories, with the fuzz and lint from woolen rugs,
throws, slipcovers, pillows. Toward the end of her life, during the
energy shortage of the seventies, my mother always kept her
thermostat at ninety degrees. Visiting, we complained that we
couldn't breathe in that heat; she told us to turn on one of the air
conditioners.

If no fresh air ever entered our house, nothing, on the other
hand, that *did* enter ever left—though once there, it might become

impossible to find. It always had an "alibi," was always in "another place" than where it belonged; this gave everyone an alibi for failings or failures. "I couldn't find a pencil." "There aren't any buttons on my dress." "The umbrellas were all gone except that broken one." There always was an excuse to do nothing.

That was the real purpose of this "indoor air," to see that one *could* do nothing—not, at least, without my mother's help and tacit permission. Suppose you wanted to drop a note to a friend—a simple task, you'd think. The house was full of pencils, for instance, yet none were in the desk; those lying about on chests or in fruit and candy bowls were broken. The sharpeners, recently in evidence everywhere, had suddenly vanished. Pens, paper, envelopes, stamps—all were equally elusive. The only solution was to ask my mother—who, with a sigh of resignation, would put down whatever she seemed to be working on, get up and begin a house-wide search. This seldom produced the desired article, but sometimes yielded a substitute which might, more or less, serve. By that time, however, an hour or two had passed. It was like opening a bank account in, or shipping a package from, a third-world bureaucracy; you finally lost impulse and gave up. Worse, you were now indebted for the time sacrificed, for your benefit, from your mother's work.

Such debts, though unpayable, could be forgiven (like international debts), especially if, meanwhile, new ones had been incurred. The unpardonable crime would have been to walk to the store across the street and buy a new one—notebook, Band-Aid, pair of socks—whatever you needed to get on with it. This would bring her to a white, silent rage; you would never hear what you had done wrong, but you might pay for months.

When I was teaching at Cornell for the small salary I've mentioned, I decided to stay in Beaver Falls all one summer with my wife and daughter. The alternative was a job on the highway; it seemed better to yield to my parents' urging and stay there, hoping to finish a literary essay which might brighten my prospects in the academic world. (I did finish the essay, but my mind was so scrambled that it took two more years to reshuffle the piece into coherence.) I was then with my second wife, Janice, a lively and strong-willed person who, I imagined, could cope with my mother—

she had never even met her, had not been trained to read and obey her unspoken commandments. After several days, my wife took some dirty clothes to a nearby cleaners. This induced a fury such as few have witnessed: my wife had not even asked which cleaner to go to, whether the clothes needed cleaning, whether they might not be washed instead, whether Mother might not take them for her. Within ten days, my wife was reduced to almost total immobility, unable to collect our dirty clothes, clean our room, carry out any of her usual activities.

My son, Russell, with whom my wife was then pregnant, was the most energetic child I have ever seen. A little like Harpo Marx: a head of golden curls, endless vitality, and completely innocent aggression; until we took strong repressive measures, he would simply walk up, sock you, then stand there grinning at how good it felt to hit people. Time and again, my mother would pick him up and put him on her lap; he became motionless as a statue. My wife's psychiatrist said, "Of course; he knew she'd eat him!" A doctor I saw many years later said, "But don't you think it's really that your son could feel how terrified *you* were and responded to that?" Good; yet how to explain that she had the same power over a small dog that didn't know any of us from Charlemagne? After two hours of incessant yapping, snarling, snapping, leaping, whirling, cartwheeling, dodging, it sat on her lap like an Egyptian stone cat or Lot's wife.

A crucial tactic within my parents' broader strategy lay in not merely helping their children—finding their socks, washing their clothes—but in buying things for them. Or simply giving them money. This proved almost unbeatable. I received improbable objects: a very costly bicycle, a mounted punching bag, toy trains, a Lionel airplane that revolved around a pylon, kettle drums, whatnot. When I got out of the Navy, they gave me an allowance *not* to take the several months of subsistence granted to discharged veterans who had not yet found a job or entered college. After I used up my GI bill, they helped keep me in school for several years. Some of this actually helped; I was and am grateful for that. Some of it, however, produced a dependency and lack of self-respect which did not seem accidental.

These methods reached full efficacy only in the time of my younger brother, Dick. I was the first child, then came two girls, Barbara and Shirley, and finally my brother, Richard—a surprise, I think, to everyone. Not only did they seem too old to have children; they seemed too alienated to have sex. By the time of his birth, however, there was more money to invest and they had perfected their techniques; they turned the full method loose on him. First they bought him expensive trinkets; then, when he lost interest in them, bought them back so that he could put the money into some new obsession. Of course he always did lose interest; these things hadn't really belonged to him. He was never allowed to pay for or to sell them to outsiders. Eventually, they became my mother's—openly—and sat amidst the general clutter accusing him of doing nothing with them.

Early on came model soldiers in amazing elaboration, then vast layouts for model trains which covered numerous tables in the game room downstairs, then drum sets, phonograph layouts and records, followed by cars—first, old Fords which could be chopped and channeled according to the fashion, then sports cars. None of the cars ran long; most were dismantled and the pieces left lying around the three-car garage.

One car did run for a while, but by then Dick had lost interest again. So there were plans to start buying him speedboats. But until the car broke down, my mother drove a black Jaguar around town, like "The Little Old Lady from Pasadena." Now and again, one of Dick's friends, gunning his engine in furious challenge, would tool up to Dick's car stopped at a red light. When he saw my mother's white sausage curls behind the steering wheel, he would slink away, abashed.

That my mother should drive at all invited catastrophe. She could barely see above the dashboard and, as she grew older, her reflexes became slow, her attention lax, and her eyesight nearly nonexistent. My son, Russell, when about ten, was riding one evening in the huge Cadillac she drove on one of Detroit's express-ways—terrifying cement expanses where cars raced four abreast at eighty miles an hour. Suddenly he realized they were going the wrong way against traffic and screamed, "Grandma! Grandma!

We're going the wrong way!" "Yes, yes," she replied placidly, "we'll have to get off at the next exit."

When she was in her seventies and even admitted that she could not distinguish small objects well, her doctor refused (despite her children's request) even to disallow renewal of her driver's license. He said that it would kill her. He apparently felt no responsibility for any schoolchildren walking those streets or riding in other cars with their families. Or perhaps she merely exerted as much power over him as she had over us.

The summer my wife and I spent in her house we made several other egregious blunders. Partly to spare her expense and work (a first blunder: our duty was to be expensive, troublesome, hence guilty) and partly to escape her cooking, we began by trying to buy and prepare some of our own food. I need not tell how briefly that effort lasted. We resigned ourselves to her meals. We decided, though, that at least we would not eat in the dining room. There, everything was dirty, cluttered, smelly. The cats slept on the table most of the day; a dark smear on the curtain betrayed where one had passed and rubbed—how many years? Besides, it was summer, the weather was lovely and the yard was full of lawn furniture. We asked if anyone would mind if we ate outside. "Why, of course not," she said, startled. We asked if anyone would like to join us; no, she answered for the group, they preferred the comforts of the dining room. So, for several months, while the indoor air grew thicker and more sullen, we had pleasant meals under a small cherry tree in the far corner. Meantime, we spent much time cleaning and ordering the yard—we needed exercise and hoped this might not offend, as any effort indoors so clearly would.

When we came back for a brief visit the following spring, we stepped out the back door and were thunderstruck; it looked like photos I'd seen of Verdun. The little cherry tree had been cut down—she said the neighbor boys kept stealing the cherries and might get hurt. Close behind the house were two large sycamores whose branches sometimes touched, and might damage, the roof. She had had two college boys take chain saws and lop off every branch at exactly half its length. Not one cut was made at a major fork, where the tree might heal; not one was tarred. It was spring;

rising sap poured from the open wounds. We could only speculate which bore my name and which my wife's.

The house was, by that time, almost unbearable to me and became more so after an altercation with my sister, Barbara. I had disagreed with my parents about something; I don't recall what. Soon afterward, my sister, usually withdrawn and mute, accosted me in the hallway, raging: "If you don't agree with what we think here, why don't you just get out—just clear out of here and never come back!" This began to seem a sensible suggestion; I decided I must accept no more money from my parents (however that might infuriate them—as it did) and never stay there more than a few days at a time.

Barbara became permanently entrenched; the family had, unquestionably, the deepest effect on her—and she, eventually, on it. The second child, two years younger than I was, she had grown to be (despite a marvelous sense of humor) shy, introverted, and neglected. My mother once became furious with a neighbor for ignoring a daughter in favor of her son. That fury scarcely disguised her own practice: both daughters, her middle children, were endured, not wanted. One Christmas, I received a very good phonograph system, while Barbara got a little nursery-type record player which produced an almost indecipherable sound. Later, I saw her crying in her room (about this inequity, I imagined) and reported this to my mother, blamefully. I was told that could not possibly be the case; instantly, the topic became unmentionable.

My sister had few friends in school and only one date in her life—with a boy my family would otherwise have scorned because he was Jewish. (In grade school, it had been a scandal that my best friend was a black boy, Elisha Grant; what if her DAR friends should see me, my mother asked, walking to school with him?) I later discovered that Barbara had had a startling fantasy life. Just as in my teens I had saved, in secret places, pictures and drawings of naked girls, I found among her papers, after her death, dozens of newspaper or magazine photographs and clippings about, of all people, Wilt Chamberlain. She had never evinced the least interest in athletics and, of course, had never acted on her fantasies, any more than upon the others she must have had—fantasies of lust, of love, of a freer life, of . . . the materials of anyone's fancies. She never wore makeup and, though she had some attractive clothes, was too shy to wear them. They all lay neatly wrapped and folded in tissue paper, just as they had come from the store, together with the boxes of high-heeled shoes, scarves, accessories. All of them too good to use.

After high school, she entered a college about fifty miles away. When, a year or two later, she had a severe asthma attack, my parents brought her home, installed her on their third floor and enrolled her in the college a block away. My wife and I, hearing this, looked at each other and said, "Well, that's the end of *her!*" We scarcely imagined how right we were.

Having graduated, she went to work in an office my father opened in Monaca, a smaller industrial town near Pittsburgh where his main office was. This lasted several years; her asthma continued; nothing happened. On her bedside stand there was always an old corncob pipe; she smoked Green Mountain Asthma Mixture which seemed to give her more relief than anything the doctors could suggest. The family physician found that she was allergic to dust, to dog and cat hair, to wool and lint. He suggested that the house be professionally cleaned, the dogs and cats disposed of, the woolen rugs, etc., replaced. My mother found all this impossible. She had always been *trying*, she protested, to clean the house; it was Barbara who was so fond of the animals and would be heartbroken without them; they couldn't afford to replace all those rugs, pillows, shawls, hangings, coats, scarves. He suggested that Barbara go to Arizona where the air was lighter and dryer, freer from dust and lint. That, too, was impossible. Barbara couldn't go alone, my mother said, and she simply hadn't time to go with her—she was needed at home to clean house and cook for my father and brother.

One morning, my brother, sleeping in the room next to Barbara's, heard her get out of bed, gasp, then fall. When he got there, she was already dying. The doctor, a decent man and an old family friend, would make no precise statement about the cause of death except that her whole system seemed to have run down and worn out. She was twenty-five. My second sister, Shirley, had just announced her engagement; I had married for the second time. It was clear that Barbara would never marry, never have a boyfriend, a job, or any life outside the family. On the morning of July Fourth, my new wife's birthday, she had found a way to declare her independence.

At her funeral, the ironies came full circle. For all the expensive display, the result seemed cheap and tawdry. The banks of flowers behind and around her coffin might have adorned a parade float of half-clad beauty queens. Given the occasion, the overwhelming sexual scent was revolting. Inside the coffin my sister was surrounded by lurid red satins and draped in a long formal gown of the sort she would neither have dared, nor consented, to wear when alive. Her face was gaudy with lipstick, rouge, eyeliner, false eyelashes. Everyone exclaimed how beautiful she looked—just like she was alive!—and commiserated with my mother on the terrible loss she had suffered.

It was worse to visit that house a year later on July Fourth, and have to sit through the mockery of a birthday party for my wife while, outside, fireworks and Roman candles resounded. If in life she had gone unnoticed, Barbara had found a way to see that everyone would notice the anniversary of her death and why she had died. In effect, she had slammed the lid on the whole family. From then on, the guilts were too deep for anyone to turn back. My father, who had adored her but had not insisted that she leave the house, never really recovered. A deep sadness, and I think a profound sense of failure, settled over him and never left till his death. In the backyard, my mother had taken wet cement and filled in the eyes—they seemed sunken in, she said—of the small stone lion which, looking very much like one of the Pekingese she'd once kept, perpetually crouched there.

As for me, I began to have asthma attacks myself whenever I went there. My wife and I decided that we must try to rescue my brother from that house and that though I had a duty to visit from time to time—actually, less each year—I must never again sleep inside the house. My mother's cats, to which I was actually quite allergic, gave me the perfect excuse to stay in a nearby motel.

III. FATHER

Even physically, my parents seemed mismatched. My mother was short, stumpy, and something of an ugly duckling. Even in childhood photos with her family she looks plain, resentful, and overshadowed by Flee, her elder sister. Flee's good looks and vivacity had taken her into higher (and, it was implied, faster) circles; my mother never forgave her.

My father was tall, slender, and, insofar as accountants dare be, dapper; he looked remarkably like Fred Astaire. Admired by women, liked by most men—his employees not least—he had a good deal of social grace. He had been a fine athlete, a local chess prodigy, had reputedly put himself through Pitt by shooting pea pool, and was now a successful businessman. Until shortly before his death he looked ten or fifteen years younger than he was. In middle age, he had to send away for his birth certificate; he had lied about his age so long that even he no longer knew.

I believe he had been a sickly child; he contracted one of the now-rare childhood diseases, perhaps diphtheria. Had it not been summer, his mother told us, he would have died. He had clung to the picket fence in their yard, she said, so his cough would not knock him down. His recovery must have been remarkable. In his teens, he worked on the ice wagon—which still existed when I was a child, carrying huge crystal blocks into every neighborhood while we children followed its dripping tailgate to cadge stray bits and chunks. Icemen were both strong and tough. Not only did they carry three-hundred-pound blocks of ice, they had to fight each other for the first newly cut blocks at the icehouse. I am told my father knew several clever holds and could throw a heavier man pretty handily. In any case, he'd been high in the pecking order and had no scars to show for it. His nose had been broken twice, but only when the heavy black ice tongs slipped off a block he was lifting and caught him in the face. This cost him severe sinus pains and several operations to remove crushed bone and cartilage, but never affected his appearance.

He must have been good at most sports, but in baseball he excelled. Here, too, the initiation was strenuous; when you joined the local team older members stuffed your mouth with chewing tobacco till all agreed on the sufficiency, then set a time to hold it. Remarkable was the explosion when that time expired. He not only passed that test, he played well. He would have tried the pros as a catcher had it not been for his one weakness, a fatal one. A catcher had to stay in his crouch and rifle the ball to second base in a flat throw that would take the pitcher's head off if he failed to duck. As you got older, he said, each of those throws took weeks off your remaining career. But that was all right; he couldn't do it even when he was young.

He tried to teach me some of his skills but I was a sore disappointment. Tied closely to my mother's apron strings, I was hopeless at most sports, especially those he was good at. Oddly enough, I got a little better at football (which he had never played); I still remember sandlot games where I got thoroughly, happily bashed and bloodied. But that's not the same as being good at it. My Uncle Stew had been a fine amateur tennis tournament player and he set out to teach me, too. I loved the game, especially the sportsmanship then expected: you didn't call doubtful points in your own favor—you called it for your opponent or played the point over. I had the best strokes in that part of the country. Sadly, I even lost to people who must never have seen a racket—in fact, especially to them. Against a fine player like Stew, I seemed almost as good. My problem was really the one Stew jokingly blamed for his infrequent losses: everything was great, only I didn't get enough points. When I couldn't call enough points against myself, I simply played poorly.

My father wanted a fighter. Each new neighborhood we moved into, I had to fight somebody in the new gang. For weeks, I let myself be picked on and bullied, then we finally squared off in some alley and flailed at each other for an hour or two. To my amazement, I won about as many as I lost, though nobody really cared about that. The boys knew I wasn't a fighter, and they could stand that better than my father could.

I couldn't play pool either—I'd seen him give three-cushion billiard demonstrations and would have given a lung to learn *that*.

Even the symbolic aggression of chess was too much for me; I studied his chess books, marveled at Alekhine, Capablanca, or Lasker, but if we sat down to play, my mind wandered. He had that gift of aggressive mental energy which kept him focused on each piece's capabilities, vulnerabilities, its place in the whole battle plan. The same gift, no doubt, kept him focused on those lines and columns of figures he juggled all day and many nights. The lack of that gift abjectly defeated me whether I was considering a Nimzovich Defence or a double-entry ledger sheet.

Not that he won all his own struggles. College boys can do you more damage, sometimes, than icemen or ballplayers. He had enrolled in Geneva College—which both my sister and I later attended—the small school about a block from the house we eventually bought. It was a strict Christian institution, run by the Reformed Presbyterian Church, a Scottish fundamentalist sect known as Covenanters; they did not smoke, drink, dance, or vote. (I once knew a Covenanter who confessed he sometimes *did* go out and sneak a vote.) Rigorously strict concerning these prohibitions, they could be strangely blind to such matters as sex, the football team's activities, and the brutality of freshman hazing. The team—once a real power that had actually beaten Harvard!—was composed of very rugged types recruited from the local mills and mining fields; they were behind much of the hazing. My father, perhaps prideful from earlier successes, was not about to be hazed—even if he had to fight the whole school. Whether they took him on one at a time or as a mob (in my days there, they specialized in mob action), I don't know. He went to the hospital; there was a considerable scandal.

After that, his parents sent him to Tarkio College, in Missouri, where he met my mother. Yet, his troubles at Geneva had not daunted him; my mother told me that one evening when they were out walking, several boys in a car made some remarks to them. He leaped into and cleaned out the carload. When his parents brought him back to finish up at Pitt, the two were separated for a year, but after his graduation, they married. I suspect his parents arranged this transfer hoping to break up the engagement; they *had* originally disapproved of his involvement with a girl from an area they thought full of Indians, outlaws, and violence. With time, they largely got over this; she did not.

My parents' marriage must have been happy at first, while they were young and poor. I can recollect, from early childhood, his coming into the room and patting her on the rump, and I seem to recall occasional embraces which looked really affectionate, almost passionate. But, by the times I can remember clearly, the cold had settled in. From time to time, he would make a gesture in her direction; this always met with icy disapproval. She never spoke a word of reproach, never said why she was angry; she just turned furiously and silently away. She kept a grudge better than anyone I've ever known.

Who knows whether any specific incident triggered this long arctic silence? Sometimes, my mother hinted at various outrages, but these seemed like Iago's "reasons" for hating Othello. She insinuated that, while she was delivering me, he had been carrying on downstairs with Flee. She suggested nothing worse than drinking, perhaps getting a little tipsy, possibly dancing. I find it hard to imagine much more. But, in her eyes, to drink at all was hell and perdition. She knew he drank with business associates—how else could he build up his business? But her convictions gave her the perfect excuse neither to accompany him to business-related luncheons and parties nor to invite his business friends home. That also gave him the perfect excuse to be away from the house whenever it suited him. It suited him more and more frequently.

After his death she once declared that the head secretary of his office had fallen in love with him: "I hadn't thought she was capable of *evil!*" she said. Such vehemence surprised me, especially since she said that my father had discharged his secretary upon learning of it. I had not thought it evil to love anyone, even if they *were* elsewhere committed; it *might* be evil for them to respond under such conditions. But she may have known more than she pretended about that long and intense love affair which, I later found, had really ended only after many years when my father finally refused to leave my mother and marry his secretary. Still, I doubt that my mother knew this; probably, like Iago, she was just good at hate and suspicion. Even if she did know, I would have thought his ultimate choice of her might have alleviated some bitterness. Or, if that bitterness had grown too deep, I'd have thought it better to leave what you cannot forgive. But at that time, I knew little about love and the delights of enduring rancor.

As time went on, he had other affairs. One night when my mother was away somewhere, he called home to say he would be working late. When he had not arrived by four in the morning, I called the police in both our hometown and in Pittsburgh to see if he had been in a traffic accident. Along about daybreak, the obvious began to occur to me. Frankly, I was relieved to find that he had other women; no one should have to subsist on my mother's meager rations of affection.

Still, I didn't want to know the details. Later, when I was visiting once from college, he invited me to lunch at his club in Pittsburgh. He arrived with a woman I had never seen—not very attractive, but well-dressed and lively. She was a businesswoman he had known since school days and with whom, it seemed, he'd had an off-and-on relation for years. I liked her, but I hated driving home and lying to my mother about our day. I wanted *him* to manage any necessary deceptions on his own. After all, by staying away so often (partly because of such affairs), he'd given us little help in handling my mother.

Despite such resentments, I preferred him to my mother—he simply was more likable. One may say that the sadist and the masochist equally create their relation; but the sadist still wields the whip and it's hard to like that. Why, then, did I not follow his example, imbibe his teaching, trace his footsteps? No doubt we all knew from the start that she was stronger, fitter to survive. Ugly enough, I admit— but children, too, recognize the real aggressors, the whip-holders, and learn to identify with them.

Simone Weil wrote, "The powerful ones of this world, if they push oppression beyond a certain point, inevitably make themselves adored." She was writing, of course, about politics, but who is to say I'm not? Where but in the family do we learn those paradigms upon which we build our later domestic and political structures? Of course, it does not bode especially well, either in love or politics, to begin our lives identifying with and adoring what we cannot admire.

At best, of course, boys are liable to oppose their fathers and I had had early clashes with mine. At bedtime when we were small, our mother would sit on our beds while we knelt at her lap to say our prayers. We said our prayers "to" her; the phrasing cannot be entirely accidental. One evening when she was away at some Ladies' Aid or DAR meeting, my father got us ready for bed and told my sister and me to say our prayers "to" him. I wanted to wait till my mother came home. He insisted; I refused. "All right, if you want a fight," he said, "you've got your fists clenched—come ahead!" I looked down, astonished, to see my fists *were* clenched; now he meant to fight me, man-to-man. I am surprised I did not faint; I was so terrified that I cannot recall what I *did* do. I suppose I gave in and treated him, for the moment, as if he were the deific figure of the family. But, like most, it was a mock conversion—and a mock victory. If anything, his need to overwhelm me convinced me of his weakness.

Against my mother, such rebellion would not have provoked any demand for submission, but rather a silent withdrawal which would have brought me, in hours, begging her to accept those rites of adoration which, by then, she would refuse to take until I demonstrated utter and abject prostration. Only when I had made manifest that this was my will, not hers, would she have reluctantly once more assumed that total domination we all demanded from her.

As I grew older, it gradually became clear that the sources of our troubles were less simple than I'd thought. My parents would take us on a trip; somewhere, sooner or later, we were bound to encounter one of those roadside stands that purvey cement birdbaths, crystal balls, painted plaster dwarfs, flamingos, reindeer, bunny rabbits. She would wander, admiring, among the aisles of these monstrosities. Often enough, though, even when she had expressed a desire for one or another of them, she would decide not to buy it—she didn't really need it. (As if anyone ever *needed* such things!) Then he would prod her, "Oh, go ahead, Helen—we can afford that." This sometimes seemed merely generous, yet why did he later complain about those very items?

When I later came back to visit, my father and I would take long evening walks to talk things over. In time, even he came to admit that he had supported, perhaps even initiated, much of her behavior. It was standard practice, of course, to urge her to take or do the things she wanted, despite her refusals or denials. We quickly became adept at reading her unspoken, her forsworn, will and forcing her to accept it. Still, he was an adult and supposedly her equal. I wanted him to enforce some order on the madness growing around them, even though common sense told me there was no way she could be controlled. She would have her way—if he wanted his home and family. Yet, he did not have to encourage what he complained against. His restraint might have helped; had it failed, her only revenge would be more coldness and scorn. How could that get much worse than it was? But he was weaker; he needed those few moments of approval or warmth his complicity could buy. She had the true invulnerability of those who can live on dominion, on adoration, without affection.

His attitudes had a less sympathetic side, though. Perhaps it's like this for anyone who lives with an alcoholic, an addict, a hypochondriac—the temptation to take gains from the other person's faults must be almost overwhelming. It was only many years later, after I had to deal with just such compensations in myself, that I realized he had encouraged her wrongdoings to put himself in the right. That motive seemed worthy, though, not of him but of her.

Still, faced with such a folie à deux, it was impossible to discern which one had started what. And I was still having troubles with both of them. He had taken a large hand in managing the children through money—it was his money, after all, and he had often initiated the financial arrangements. They had kept me in school, studying poetry, for years. When troubles arose, they had bailed me out. Though it had been understood that these were to be loans, when I tried to pay them back both parents acted hurt and offended. They insisted on buying me more things, putting me further in debt. I protested, weakly I suspect, that it would be better if they saved their money—someday I might really need it.

Eventually, such a day came: my first marriage broke up, I had support payments, lawyer's bills, and Paul Engle, my director at the university, had, without telling me, scratched me off his fellowship list. Now I needed my father's help. When I went to him, he hesitated, "But what if we don't want to support something like this? Is that it—you just name it and we pay for it? After all, what did *you* ever do for me?" I withdrew the request, took a job in a hospital, and entered psychiatric therapy. This clash, the therapy, and my sister's death led quickly to a decision that I must cut many of my ties to the family.

Nonetheless, I visited sometimes and still had long talks with my father. By that time, some part of me really did despise him—for his weakness, his failure to rescue any of us from my mother's grip, his subtle manipulations of us. (I began to understand our country's financial dealings with smaller and weaker countries; he would have made a superb diplomat.) Still, even as I feared and hated my mother, yet knew I had no choice but to love her, so I had no choice but to like, perhaps love, him. I certainly wanted him alive and well; he, meantime, was aging fast. Barbara's death hung over him like smog; he finally began to look his age, near sixty; small symptoms which might suggest cancer began to appear.

His younger brother, Stew, had a heart attack and died before he did. One year, my father told me his doctor, his lawyer, and his barber had all died. "I can get another doctor and lawyer," he joked, "but where can I find a decent haircut now?" On one of our walks, he said a small growth had been removed from his left temple, but had proved benign. "I almost thought my troubles were over," he said. Then he added, "But you don't get to my age without saving enough sleeping pills to take care of your problems." Though this seemed an admirable resolve, I didn't want it to come to that.

At least once I said openly that I feared for his life if he stayed there. His only recourse would be illness—only if people were ill could she forgive them. Then she would care for them with every loving kindness though they would never recover. After a long argument, he finally said, "But don't you see: this is The Snodgrass House. How can I just leave it?" I was reminded of Freud's lament when they came to rescue him from Nazi Germany, and of the rejoinder, "But don't you see, Doctor, that your country has already left *you*?"

I did not make the rejoinder. The blatancy of the lie suggested it served a real need and would be defended. But I was becoming more and more furious with lies. I grew still angrier as he grew weaker and the cancer finally appeared. When I next saw him, his arm was in a sling; the next time it was gone. He *was* letting himself be buried a piece at a time, letting her nurse him to death. In time, I heard, he was to lose a leg, yet they were planning a big trip to Jamaica as soon as he "recovered." Of course, he never did.

For years my fury at these lies, at his failure to take the pills, continued. Then my brother, who had more contact with the family than I, revealed that just at the time my father fell ill, the economy had suffered a severe slump; confined to the hospital, he had not been able to manage his own portfolio and had lost heavily. Carefully playing his way back into the market, he had stretched out his life so that he could leave enough money for my mother to finish her life comfortably. If he had taken the pills, we would have had to care for her—and I was the oldest child. Again, I had misjudged my father.

Sometimes, he judged himself and his life as harshly. Shortly after he bought his first Cadillac, he told me a joke. Its scene is the burial of a famous tycoon. A huge derrick is lowering, in place of a coffin, the rich man's Cadillac into an open grave. Behind the wheel sits the tycoon, embalmed, surrounded by lilies, gladioli, chrysanthemums, and unopened bottles of champagne. At one side, away from the well-dressed mourners, sit two Black grave diggers. One says to the other, "Man, that's what I call really living!"

Much of my mother's worst behavior abated once he was dead. His funeral, however, was not one of her nobler performances. As we were to leave for the undertaker's, she came downstairs in a white woolen suit and a soiled white blouse. Not quite daring to say such an outfit would be suitable for a wedding, I did ask if she might not want to change into something more appropriate. "Oh, but Father always loved white so much," she said; "I'm doing this in honor of him!" Then she took my arm, prodding me to lead her out the front door. On the steps she paused, "Wait, maybe I should go back. I'm not wearing any underpants. But no, it's probably not necessary." I began to understand why Blake had written:

The truth that's told with bad intent
Beats all the lies you can invent.

IV. THE HOUSE OF SNODGRASS

"Both," said my father, whenever alternatives arose, "are worse." If, for any reason, I mentioned a girl's name, he asked, half-kidding, "What does her father do?" Arguing that our household had fewer restrictions than most, he declared, "There's only one rule: whatever you want, you can't have it and whatever you're doing, stop it." That this was already *two* rules, which between them mandated absolute stasis and despair, was only part of the joke.

He was right. If only *one* alternative were worse, it would soon cease being an alternative. Besides, to those favored by the status quo, even if both alternatives are bad, the mere fact of alternatives, of "bothness," is worse yet: that could lead to choice and change. There go your neighborhood, your values, your advantages. And what can so threaten the status quo as for the young to choose outsiders, the children of those who work at something else? Our amiable Uncle Stew, learning that my brother was dating a girl from a barber's family—Italian and, worse, Catholic—rose up like an old-fashioned, wrathful tyrant to forbid Dick his house.

As for our household's rules, we, like modern states which call themselves "free," had subtler methods of deterrence and enforcement. My mother had marked out her empire, then blenderized everything inside its borders, rendering choice unthinkable. Our walls displayed a fantastic mélange of unmatching objects and improbable imitations thereof, things of every style, period, fad or fashion, taste or lapse therefrom. Tapestries of implausible scenes from Louis XIV's court hung beside vast, commercially reproduced watercolor scenes of Venice. Elbowing these were prettified copies of Frans Hals' paintings, portraits on velvet of blonde little girls, Middle Eastern coffee cabinets, magazine renderings of dewy-eyed dogs and cats, myriad reproductions of Pennsylvania Dutch trivets, sets of chimes and gongs. Every flat surface was crammed with Egyptian cobra-shaped candy trays, ceramic dwarves, copies of ancient Greek vases, Depression glassware, Bavarian china, plastic cups and saucers, painted lead soldiers and their artillery, rubber

Godzillas. On the mantels, framed photographs of family members stood in such proliferation that one could not distinguish who *was* represented where.

This was not accidental; a similar policy obtained toward the persons shown. Inside the family, my mother had made one basic distinction: boys might be forgiven; they could make names for themselves, so glorifying her. Girls were merely work. To belie this leaning, all other discriminations (or the recognition that one always makes discriminations) were forbidden, downright criminal. Preference might imply that something contained was not ennobled merely by the fact of containment. Our house was like Carl Sandburg's song where "all cigarettes are milder than all other cigarettes"; when both are worse, everything is better than everything else. On these democratic principles of dogmatic indiscriminacy, my parents—she who clearly did not want children, he who vanished whenever possible from his own Panglossian household—set out to found a house, a dynasty, a name.

"We revolutionaries," said Dr. Goebbels, "have always known the future; it is only the past that has to be established." When my mother joined the DAR—which, like the Ladies' Aid Society or the Bible Study Group, she would attend only during years when she'd been elected President or Program Chairman—she had to search out her antecedents. Establishing a past for us soon obsessed her. She wrote hundreds of letters, spent days in libraries reading family histories, newspapers, diaries, any sort of document which could prove that her family had immigrated earlier than those foreigners from the poorer parts of town.

Her name had been Jessie Helen Murchie. "Blessed are the Murchieful...," intoned my father, perhaps implying that she spent more time researching her own name than his, which would identify the line from then on. Still, she did write in for one of those improbable Coats of Arms which some outfit in North Carolina promised to "provide." The idea that *any* such device had ever existed was ludicrous. Yet a Coat of Arms did arrive in the mail, flaunting three large black birds, jackdaws apparently, as our heraldic beasts. Should we display that above our own ceremonial board in the dining room, lighted by its big, blue candles, bent and drooping over double with the artificial heat? Why not a flag as well?—Elsie's panties, say, or one of those sour-smelling wash-cloths which replaced them on the towel rack. Our motto, effulgently embroidered there, might read, "Washrag, cleanse thyself!" Or even, "Panties, clothe thyself!"

My father not only funded the present, so insuring the future; he played a comic Hegel to my mother's grim Bismarck, providing the philosophical veneer which could justify her rule and make loyalty not merely expedient, but noble. When, for instance, I talked of changing that name which had cost me so much trouble in school, he replied that it didn't matter what your name was, only what you made of it.

That seemed a counsel of despair: my schoolmates were not about to be assuaged by such sophistries and there seemed little likelihood I could make of my name anything which would please either one, much less both of us. The name was honorable enough in its origins: "snod" is merely Scots for tidy or trimmed. One of my ancestors must have owned a large lawn or, more likely, had to cut someone else's. Perhaps he was leader of a crew of mowers—humble but decent beginnings. Soon, though, we fell to the British who owned vast lawns, but in whose dialect the name became absurd.

What multitudes have reveled in taking our name in vain! In the early humorous writing of Mark Twain we find not only Thomas Jefferson Snodgrass and Quintus Curtius Snodgrass, but Zylobalsamum Snodgrass and Spinal Meningitis Snodgrass. Once, mysteriously, he refers to "the celebrated author . . . Snodgrass." Over the years, the name has lost none of its evocative powers. Our Sunday comics featured a bloated windbag: Senator Snodgrass. My father chuckled at that; he was less amused by a radio adventure program where the hero's pet monkey carried our much abused cognomen.

Probably the only poem on whose excellence my father and I could agree was one by Ogden Nash that divided all humanity into the Swozzlers and the Snodgrasses. The Swozzlers—as might be expected of corrupt, greedy, deceitful, "ruthless egotists like they"—rule the world. In contrast, "A Snodgrass is a kind, handsome, intelligent person, who . . ." Who gets the bejesus stomped out of him. That may explain why most Snodgrasses I had met or heard about were closet Swozzlers.

There *had* been some earlier, reputable Snodgrasses. A friend once sent me a sermon, published in the 1870s, by the Rev. Dr. W. D. Snodgrass—perhaps the W. D. Snodgrass my family had applied for but who had appeared a century too soon. Again, after my poetry readings, listeners with a background in the sciences often rush up to ask, in voices hushed with awe, if I might be related to Robert Evans Snodgrass, the famous entomologist and expert on— I am not making this up—grasshoppers.

Few have done so well by the name. My father knew a man who had witnessed one of the three greatest blunders in baseball. The situation was classic: the last and deciding game of the 1912 World Series, last half of the 10th, the Giants ahead but Boston at bat with the bases loaded, the count gone to 3 balls, 2 strikes. The batter popped a high fly to Fred Snodgrass in center field, an easy out. Our namesake needn't have moved his feet; he could have turned around and caught the thing in his hip pocket; he stood for what seemed hours, glove raised. The ball hit him in the chest and bounced so far that, had it gone the right way, the 2nd baseman could have caught it.

Others of our name have found their niche in sports. While a student at Iowa, I met a man who was part of the same troupe as Elvira Snodgrass, the Lady Wrestler. A former guard on the Iowa football squad, he was not noted for delicacy of expression. Still he told me, "I didn't like going into stores or nothing with her, she was so big and loud. She had a cowboy hat and boots and—man!—did she ever have a foul mouth on her!"

In the Navy, sailors sometimes asked if I knew the Snodgrass who had played the piano on the weekly radio program from a prison in the Midwest. This Snodgrass had had a devout following and, I was told, many were saddened by his parole. Such grief was short-lived, however—within months he was back behind bars and able, once again, to gladden the land with harmony.

Later, still another Snodgrass admitted he had been secretly coached for a television program, *The $64,000 Question,* so as to seem a veritable polymath, answering incredibly difficult questions and winning large sums. This scandal brought us little direct obloquy since it was overshadowed by the more spectacular confessions of Charles Van Doren, the son of a highly respected poet. This, of course, did little to improve my father's feelings about poets in the family.

English literature could already boast two Snodgrasses, both fictitious and both poets. In *The Pickwick Papers*, of course, is Mr. Augustus Snodgrass, a sensitive person seen, in my illustrated edition, standing in a garden, notepad in hand, waiting to take dictation from a songbird overhead. On the other hand, in *A Cool Million* by Nathanael West, is Sylvanus Snodgrasse, a Southern fascist who heads a band of pickpockets, runs a freak show in an attic (actually a front for the dissemination of subversive propaganda) and who, finally, barely escapes being lynched. All this should have warned my father.

He, meantime, did what he could to make our name, if not serious, respectable. First, there were letterheads and office doors reading, B. D. Snodgrass, CPA. Then he hired his brother and settled on Snodgrass & Snodgrass, CPAs. The main office was still in Pittsburgh; Stew ran the smaller one in Beaver Falls; my sisters, first Barbara, then Shirley, ran the third. My father wanted to open a fourth in Beaver, a more elegant, Waspish city, but who would run it? And who was to take over this empire after his death or retirement? Everyone seemed to be looking, sidelong, in my direction.

He had once asked me, as part of the ongoing plot, to read a tax book for him. He hadn't time, he said, to prepare for an upcoming court appearance; would I read one of the relevant cases and sum up how it related to his? I think I tried; I hope I tried; but I more fervently hope he didn't much rely on anything I told him. Tax books are written in a language that makes Hittite cuneiform tablets seem like a good read. This language prided itself on every fault of which he later accused (with equal justice) my early poems: deliberate obscurity, senseless repetition, pretentiousness, archaism. The scheme backfired: I would have suffered any hardship rather than endure exile into lands where that language was native.

My father was more diligent, I confess, in trying to enter my world than I his. He had never been scornful of learning as such, or of those who, outside the family, pursued it. When I described certain brilliant classes of mine at the University of Iowa, he countered by telling—with a genuine, if surprised, pleasure— about a seminar he had taken at Pitt that devoted a whole semester to *King Lear*.

In middle age he set out to complete his own education. Was he competing with me, now a perpetual student? Had he encoun- tered some tradition where the head of a family or business was expected to be a man of learning and culture? Was he influenced by the radio's *University of Chicago Round Table* or *Information Please* which featured such genuine polymaths as John Kieran, Oscar Levant, and F.P.A., Franklin P. Adams? In any case, he undertook the archetypal comic strip task: "Bringing Up Father." He went about this just as the archetypal accountant might: he read, from begin- ning to end, checking off each in turn, the University of Chicago's list of the world's 100 Best Books.

Now I would discover him in the living room reading not a tax book, not even a chess book, but Bertrand Russell's *History of Philosophy*, Frazer's *The Golden Bough*, or one of Will and Ariel Durant's well-written, beautifully illustrated and unexceptionably orthodox histories of civilization. Reading, he kept in hand one of his mechanical pencils and a straightedge with which he meticu- lously underlined passages or added marginal comments in a neat, legible hand. Sometimes, as a straight-edge, he used a folded strip of paper on which he also noted unfamiliar words or phrases that, like the odds and ends my mother collected, might come in handy. Now and again I still find, when reading one of his books, a strip which lists:

> extrapolate
> innocuous desuetude
> syncretism
> a force so malign as to partake of the godhead

and so on in a straight column down the page. Of course, these words and phrases—like my mother's vast squirrelings—never *did* prove usable.

In time, he had to read not only art histories, like Elie Faure's, but also novels, plays, possibly some poetry. He was fascinated by the Russian novels, especially *The Brothers Karamazov, Crime and Punishment* and Turgenev's *Fathers and Sons*. He urged me to read the last of these, a request I thought as suspect as that involving the tax case. I assumed he thought me like Bazarov, the rebellious, nihilistic son, and that if I read the book, I might mend my ways. Yet, when I *did* read it, I found no such resemblance; Bazarov flatly scorned the sort of high-flown ideals which I was always spouting. In fact, my father himself—with his talk of hardheaded practicality—seemed more like Bazarov. Again, I was missing the point somewhere.

In my own middle age, I became equally unable to read a book without a pen (usually red) in hand. I underline freehand; my meandering lines cancel out the text almost as often as they underscore it. They seem also to cancel it from my memory: now and again, having long felt guilty for failure to read some classic, I pick it up to find, there, extensive red underlinings and marginal comments (some quite embarrassing) in my own hand.

That suggests a crucial difference. My father's exact and exacting line meant that something added up. As a result, his reading never changed his attitude or significantly affected any decision of his. Yet, he grasped every volume clearly and, years later, quoted passages with astonishing accuracy.

When I underline a passage, it instantly disappears into an abiding chaos, not unlike the jumble of my mother's house, inside my skull and rib cage. Similarly, when I make a poem, I erect a column of words much like those words on my father's page markers or the figures on his balance sheet. Like him, I intend in this an act of inventory and mastery; sadly, it confers control only over a range of cortical response, pretends to no dominion except within a sort of ceremonial light-show of the intellect and emotions. Auden was right: poetry makes nothing happen. If, under its column, you can draw a line and calculate some simple, balancing answer, your books have been jimmied.

The poem does not drive out chaos; it thumbs its nose at it. How better to confirm its almost overwhelming presence? Ideas, chess, the arts—they offer us forms of play, outlets for mental energies which yearn, desperately, to tie up the world and pull its teeth. No matter: the world does not read the rules; whatever our tactics, we will lose. Only the arts admit—no; proclaim—that despite whatever prowess we may achieve, we're still at the mercy of our mortality, of our frequently foolish passions. No wonder artists are disliked. Reveling in mastery over the world's details, they show us, finally, our helplessness before its totality—not just that we have the wrong ideas but that there are no right ones. If it had an answer, it wouldn't be a problem.

My father, like Plato, thought the artist dangerous because he keeps mentioning matters, like his own passions and perceptions, that the society wants to ignore. I thought the artist valuable for the same reason. Chances are, both of us were worse, each more wrong than the other.

Both of us had been reading Renaissance plays, poems, and songs that ridiculed and vilified fathers. Maybe poetry *does* make something happen. Encouraged to oppose their fathers openly, the more gifted sons have often had to become outsiders, to work at something else and to succeed at that before they could set up their own families. We have not only provided alternatives for sons, we have mandated them. If this has offered the culture marvelous creative energies, it has provided no less impressive neuroses, tension, and unhappiness. Change has become so endemic that many live in a constant state of uprootedness and culture shock. Yet this is only to say that our homegrown conflict brings us some measure of flexibility, some range of options and alternatives as the pendulum of ideas and interests swings back and forth with the generations.

Who, at this point, could draw up a balance sheet on what part the arts have played in the process, on whether both fathers and sons have been better or worse? Still, like most of us, fathers remember most vividly the times they have been attacked and are not likely to think well of forces which they see as fraternizing with the enemy: change.

Fathers feel they carry the banner of civilization. Wives and children, especially if those fathers have brought them security and affluence, are likely to have other notions. My father had little fear of revolt from my mother—she already ruled him absolutely. The children were another matter. Too timid for open rebellion, my sister had defeated him by dying in that uniform of ideas the family had designed and which had become like a second skin. No doubt any creature that developed an armor too protective might smother if it could not shed that skin with growth.

Once Barbara was gone, my younger sister, Shirley, was moved up to fill that gap in the formation; she was given Barbara's bedroom, her job in Father's office—suddenly admitted not only to the executive washroom, but to personhood. People are likeliest to revolt not when most oppressed but after a first step upward. Shirley's promotion filled her with an extreme, if unfocused, rage. Perhaps to be treated as interchangeable, perhaps to find that her earlier neglect arose neither from the nature of the universe nor from any inadequacy of her own—in any case, for some time you approached at your own risk. This must have been a major problem in tact for my father. Circumstances came to his aid: Shirley's husband could not find the teaching position for which he had trained, my father could offer him, too, a position in the firm. The survivors' interests narrowed and converged.

A deeper irony lay in my father's relation to me. Fathers are former sons, and many have, within them still, a rebellious child tacitly supporting the next generation's plots against them. James Billington has shown that the French Revolution was sparked by young idealistic theorists, working inside the Palais Royale which belonged to Philip of Orleans, cousin of Louis XIV. The Russian Revolution was hatched by a similar group centered in the student building of St. Petersburg's Imperial Practical Technological University—again under the auspices of those authorities whom they would overthrow. In the '60s and '70s, many a father delivered his children to protests or sit-ins before driving on to his own work at the Pentagon. With my father's acquiescence, my mother pulled strings that catapulted me into the Writing Workshops at the University of Iowa. As he had once paid for my music lessons, he went on paying for my education in poetry.

Once, on the radio program *Information Please*, John Kieran's son submitted a question which stumped his father. Kieran bounced back instantly with a scrambled quotation: "How sharper than a thankless tooth to have a serpent child!" My father must have loved that moment—and not only because he had once studied *King Lear*. All his order and precision were being diverted into the support of chaos and waste by my mother; he was nourishing in his bosom a serpent, an artist—me.

V. ARTIST AND BUSINESSMAN

"Why don't you say what you mean?" my father asked. A just complaint—my early poems, struggling for complexity, for breadth and depth, were merely obscure. Still, if I *had* said what I meant, he'd have liked that even less. What he meant was: "Why don't you stop meaning?"

Any close contact with the arts filled my father, like so many American men, with repugnance and a barely disguised fear. How could he have liked them? Demanding strict truth on his ledger sheets, he required evasions everywhere else. He worked among men who dealt in half-truths, euphemisms, diplomacies, advertisements; he headed a house where truth was forbidden more sharply than obscenity; every Sunday he drove us to celebrate a belief that had little other effect upon his life. His mind was far too keen to feel anything but scorn for that church's vision—or for that schlock art which met his demands. Courageous against every physical threat, he fled, panic stricken, from poems, paintings, music which did not conform to his preconceptions, to the things he hoped he meant.

Perhaps my mother had less reason to distrust the arts; everyone thought they, like morality, belonged to the woman's sphere. She, when young, had wanted to play the violin but her family—her father was a United Presbyterian minister in the Midwest—had never been able to afford an instrument and lessons. So, as I began to drift into music, I could act out her ambitions. And I could frustrate her husband.

Until I was in my teens, classical music was unheard of, or certainly unheard, in our house—as in most respectable homes thereabouts. In our town, the only exception was a dentist and his wife, who directed plays; together, they formed half of a string quartet. But they were Jews; what could you expect? Still, middle-class houses usually had a piano and someone always took nominal music lessons.

We had only one relative actively involved with the arts, my father's uncle, Bryce Fogel—my grandmother's brother, but scarcely older than my father. The name Bryce was a more elegant version of my father's (and his father's) name, Bruce—a name that echoed with tales of warrior-princes, brigand-heroes, cattle thieves. It must have relieved my parents that Bryce lived at a distance—in New York where he performed as a baritone, earned part of his living as an accompanist and piano teacher, and apparently cadged the rest from rich friends or patrons; he was homosexual.

Whenever Bryce visited my great-aunts Goldie and Erma, his mother and aunt who lived about sixty miles away, he also came for a family dinner with my grandparents, then was to be coaxed to give an "impromptu" concert afterward. He sang just what he happened to be studying at the time—no matter; whatever he performed would have seemed equally deadly to us. At one such *liederabend* (I really think this occurred at *our* house) he sang through Moussorgsky's *Sunless Cycle*. We would as gladly have listened to brake drums clanging for an hour.

My only clear recollection of that evening concerns my father's sister, Catherine, who had pretensions to society and culture, and who said, "Oh, Bryce, you must tell them how *you* say 'Dah-BOO-sie.'" He dutifully did so, demonstrating the French diction taught by his current singing coach, then proceeded to coach us children in the "new" pronunciation of that name—as if we had ever pronounced it before!

We thought this aunt a snob; we had no idea what to think of Bryce. I suppose we were impressed by his strong, aquiline features, his wildly curling hair and elegant carriage. Nonetheless, we whispered a story my father had told of visiting Bryce in Greenwich Village, where he lived in squalor. As the two of them walked out into the street, a rat had dashed across the sidewalk in front of them; Bryce had stepped upon and crushed it. I cannot help imagining that he did this without a sidelong glance or a break in his stride and conversation—like Cyrano skewering a bully. My father was not impressed. What did he want Bryce to do—shout for the police or climb a telephone pole screaming? Ignore the whole thing as unmentionable, just as he did? No; he wanted Bryce to do *everything* just as he did—above all, move out of there and get a "regular" job.

My father, strangely, had been only slightly less apostate in his own family. For them, as for my mother's family, there were only two honorable professions: medicine and the ministry. He was expected to emulate *his* father, a general practitioner, or his uncle, another United Presbyterian minister. When he decided, instead, to become an accountant, his mortified parents refused to pay for further schooling. He financed that himself at menial bookkeeping jobs with Price, Waterhouse and Westinghouse Electric. Meantime, he and my mother lived in Wilkinsburg, a rundown suburb of Pittsburgh, where I was born. Things must have been pretty tight; even after he was reconciled with his family and moved back to Beaver Falls, for several years we shared a duplex with another family in a scruffy neighborhood.

I sometimes wished those struggles had made my father more understanding toward my choice of vocation. Clearly, he had proved his point. Alas, that made him no readier to concede any such point to me. That may be just, though: I can't guarantee that his disapproval wasn't part of the arts' attraction for me. However that may be, my early encounters with the muses were scarcely triumphant; I became—and for almost ten years remained—that least lovable of mortals, a beginning violinist. And this befell me in the most absurd fashion imaginable.

When I was perhaps six or eight, my mother took me to some sort of musical show, perhaps a visiting troupe from one of the Pittsburgh radio stations, where I'd been fascinated by violins. Not by their sound, by their mechanics. Imagining that the bow hair (I did not even know it *was* hair) passed *beneath* the strings, I wondered how players got it there, then detached the bow when finished. I probably expressed this as an interest in playing the instrument—after all, if I played I would discover how the bow and strings connected. It little occurred to me that hard work or concentration might be involved in learning to play—throughout my childhood and extended adolescence, I suffered from the delusion that one did such things by just buying an expensive piece of equipment, then *using* it. Before I knew what had happened, I had a violin and let myself be sentenced to years of frustrating and futile lessons rather than admit the nature of my interest. I still think with embarrassment of my teacher, a shy, gawky man who had shattering headaches and, during our weekly torture sessions, tugged frantically at his collar as if he were being throttled.

After I played at several church functions—which, to hear my mother, might have been Carnegie Hall recitals—even I began to notice what wretched sounds I was producing. I switched to the piano but that was little better: here, again, bad habits and laziness (that is, lack of real interest) guaranteed that I would never achieve even mere competence. Several more years of alternate drudgery and neglect passed.

Then, in high school, like Saul on the road to Damascus, I had a revelation. You could say that I fell in love, though there was nothing overtly sexual about it. Everyone called him "Flash"—his name was Leo Hamilton, he played tympani and was student conductor of the high school band and orchestra, both surprisingly good. He was older than most of us, having often moved about the country with his mother. His parents were divorced (unheard of, then), his mother managed a country club not far away (equally unheard of), he drove to school (again, unheard of) in an aged, rickety but picturesque Model A Ford. He was even slimmer and more elegant than my father, carried himself with startling snap and energy. Very much a figure in the school, his air of difference, of daring, of ability, had already brought him several devoted disciples. He was sleeping with both members of a set of twins, one of whom was beautiful and the other, he reported, passionate.

I soon became his leading acolyte, started taking tympani lessons and cultivating a taste for what my hero called "orchestral violence"—music with a great deal of brass and percussion. Every day after school we hurried to the local appliance store which, in the back, sold a limited stock of classical recordings. Out of the goodness of her heart (or, perhaps, mere loneliness) the lady who ran this section accepted our fiction that we were really thinking of buying all those old, vulnerable shellac 78s. Every day, we lugged these into the little listening booths and spun hour after hour of Tschaikovsky, Liszt, Beethoven, Wagner. I don't suppose it made too much difference if we did wear them out; no one bought them, anyway.

Only once was Flash invited to our house for dinner—one of the strangest events of my childhood. The meal was reasonably edible (perhaps reflecting my mother's approval); it seemed a pleasant occasion. Then my father did something that I still have trouble believing: he told a dirty joke—and a poor one at that. Turning to Flash, he asked, "Did you hear the one about the stewardess who said, 'Would you like some of my TWA coffee or my TWA tea?'" Perhaps he meant to show that he was a "regular guy"; perhaps he was testing whether _Flash_ was; perhaps he meant to trick him into a damning concurrence. Flash and I later wondered if he had understood his own joke; in any case, we both acted as if _we_ had not. My mother shook and glared; we finished the meal in frightened silence. The price would be exorbitant; payments would begin at once and last for years.

Whatever his motives in this contretemps, my father must have thought little would come of my musical involvements. Once or twice, he drove me to hear concerts by the Pittsburgh Symphony and he paid for my lessons with the tympanist of that orchestra. In time, World War II getting under way, Flash joined the Marines hoping to get into one of the wartime bands; I moved into his place, first as tympanist, then student conductor. I once conducted a rehearsal of Beethoven's Third, an experience sure to generate delusions of omnipotence. My first year at Geneva College near my home, almost all the guys had gone to war; we _did_ have a (mostly girl) chorus, which I briefly conducted. That, too, encouraged delusions.

After my own two years in the Navy, though, it was clear I had to get out of music. At eighteen, I had been behind; at twenty, I was hopeless. Besides, my own virginity was weighing on me; I was desperate to get married. Still, I thought I belonged somewhere in the arts. A new order of folly—the notion that I had at least the basic material, the English language—led me to think I might be able to write plays. The GI bill took me to the State University of Iowa. My plays were terrible; my teachers in the theatre were no help. I drifted into the Poetry Workshop—though I had, at first, no desire to write poetry, here at least I found teachers I could admire: they knew something about one of the arts.

For a while I sent my parents copies of my poems with copious explanatory notes, hoping to gain their approval. I live in dread that some of those notes may yet surface with my self-serving pleas for those poems' significance. In time, I realized that my parents not only didn't know, they didn't care whether the poems were any good: she would praise them because *her son* had written them, he would dislike them for the same reason; better keep them to myself.

No doubt my father thought the war and marriage would mature me—that is, make me agree to take over his thriving business. He waited while I went through undergraduate school, took an MA, then an MFA and started on a PhD. Though I told him this would help me support myself while writing poems, I don't think I ever seriously believed I could get the doctorate. I merely wanted to stay in school. The teaching market outside was bleak; meantime, I really was learning something about poetry and thought I had found something I could do. In fact, I was learning about all the arts; the atmosphere at Iowa was saturated with them. I have never again felt so nourished by the brilliance of those around me. Meantime, I lived on assistantships and my wife's earnings as a school teacher and hospital clerk.

And on my father's handouts. Though he did continue to support me in a choice he disapproved of, he had by no means given up hope. Even after I had a daughter, had been divorced and remarried, had a stepdaughter, then a son; even after I pried myself out of graduate school and could squeak out a living as a teacher at Cornell, at Rochester, then at Wayne State in Detroit, his hopes persisted. Several fellowships did not entirely disabuse him. When my first book appeared, however, he became seriously threat-ened—this really might confirm me in a life of folly. "For God's sake," he said, "when are you going to give up all this nonsense and settle down to something serious? Don't you see that you'll never amount to a hill of beans with this sort of thing?" Several weeks later, the book was awarded the Pulitzer Prize for 1960.

Even then I knew that such prizes meant nothing about the quality of my work. Much later I learned of the actual political maneuvers and pressures behind my own award. Most of the judges— newspapermen who knew nothing of poetry—had tried to force Louis Untermeyer, the chief judge, to choose a book, any book, of light verse. With the help of Caleb Bingham, a Southern editor who *did* read poetry, Untermeyer had managed to give it to me instead.

Walter F. Kerr, the drama critic, sometimes remarked, "Two wrongs don't make a right; they make an award." His son Gilbert wrote me many years later about the repercussions of this particular award on his family. His mother, the playwright Jean Kerr, had tried to convince her friend Phyllis McGinley that she, McGinley, was likely to win the Pulitzer that year. When the award was announced, she received from her friend this verse:

> Where poets romp, the fields are green
> Although it's rather odd grass;
> Repeat this slowly with me, Jean:
> "There is a man named Snodgrass . . . !"

Repercussions elsewhere were sometimes less amusing. Picking my book cost Untermeyer the judgeship; the following year he was ousted and the prize given to Miss McGinley for another book, which had a preface by W. H. Auden.

Though I then knew none of these details, I strongly suspected that excellence might not always be the chief desideratum in apportioning of awards. Even so, this one changed the tenor of my life. Overnight, I could find teaching posts at schools that until then wouldn't have accepted me even as a student; magazines that had already turned down everything I'd written wrote asking for anything I might have on hand. Dozens of schools wanted me to give readings at startling fees; new fellowships loomed; women who had found me surpassingly dull the week before, now glowed with reconsideration.

I had already watched friends who, after years of hoping and praying, finally got a fellowship—and almost instantly fell apart. I was determined this would not happen to me. Yet the shallow therapy which had rescued me from a failing first marriage and from two years of writers' block was obviously coming unglued. My second wife and I, who had been affectionate and happy while dirt-poor, both turned selfish and faithless; my writing was drying up again. I entered a second, deeper psychoanalysis with a basic Freudian in Detroit. Among his first words were, "Well, there's one thing your money won't buy you: poverty."

The repercussions inside my family were equally distressing. For my mother, the award was a triumph—the final proof of her excellence as a mother. As I had come seriously to doubt that excellence, the prize got even harder to stomach. She had supported, emotionally, my choice of the arts and my efforts there. That support, however, had motives I could not share—I wanted no further part in my parents' struggle. Worse, her support, whatever it proved about her excellence, did not intend mine. If she had once wanted me to play the violin, she had never encouraged me to practice. It is easier to want your children to share your unfulfilled ambitions than to help them fulfill them. Since her praise finally enjoined mediocrity, it might well be more dangerous than my father's disregard.

Against my father, living well *was* the best revenge. The award did get him off my back. But just as it brought me friends whose true colors appeared only when my luck changed, so it insured that when the explosion with my father finally came, it would be all the uglier for that. Of the friends or loved ones my good fortune distressed or turned against me, I can most easily sympathize with his motives. Once and for all, he lost the heir apparent to his business. Beyond, he must accept a son who lived outside his social circumstances and philosophical acceptances. Worse yet, I had not had to give up my own inclinations, as he had had to give up baseball and chess. I had taken upon myself to say forbidden things and had not only escaped punishment, I had been rewarded.

I was given this prize chiefly for a cycle of poems, "Heart's Needle," about what I then took to be the loss of my daughter in my first divorce. In those poems, I had taken (without being aware of it) my father's advice and had "said what I meant." At this late date, it is a little hard to recall how wrongheaded, or downright revolutionary, those poems seemed to many in the '50s and '60s. We had been taught to write poems in an obscure and symbol-laden language on "significant" subjects: the loss of myth in our time, the decay of civilization. I found that if I was to write at all, I had to address what I really cared about, in a language as direct as I could muster. Since the artist's life was probably a mistake anyway, I might as well make a big mistake, not go on making small, derivative ones.

Robert Lowell, who had become a sort of substitute father, grew concerned for me: "You mustn't write this kind of tear-jerking stuff," he said. "You've got a brain!" When, later, he himself came to write on somewhat similar subjects, he got the same kind of censure from *his* mentor, Allen Tate. For once, my father was at one with general critical opinion. My poems had followed his advice, but he certainly hadn't meant that they should talk about anything not discussed in polite circles.

About a year after the award, the State Department sent me to give poetry readings in Belgium and at the Edinburgh Festival; the next year, after a plan to send me to Russia had fizzled out, they proposed to send me to several smaller Eastern European countries—Bulgaria, Romania, Hungary, possibly Yugoslavia and Czechoslovakia—then on to Austria, Germany, France, and Portugal. I had never been in Europe, did not know the language, currency, or even the capitals of many of those countries. But how could one say no?

This trip, on which I could not afford to take my wife, cost me my second marriage and renewed problems with my parents. It also cost me considerable problems of conscience: I was deeply opposed to American foreign policy. The trip was well worth those problems. In the Balkans, I had a genuine sense of discovery. I had read too much about Paris, Vienna, Berlin—they seemed "used." Sofia, Bucharest, Budapest weren't like anything I'd heard about. These peoples, once a gray blob called "Iron Curtain Countries," were as varied and fascinating as newly discovered species of tropical birds. The Bulgarians, dedicated Slavs, were serious, stolid, self-effacing, put their lives into their landscape, loved Communism, loved the Russians; the Romanians thought themselves descended of the ancient Dacians and the Roman settlers, were lively, colorful, doggedly Latin and demonstrative, loved Communism and hated the Russians; the Hungarians were Magyars, every man for himself.

These people we had thought dullards, lacking in culture, taste, or ability, fit only to slave in our factories or drudge on highways and railroads, actually had histories, cultures, traditions far older and richer than ours. In each country I made lifelong friends; in Hungary and Romania I started translating songs and ballads from their store of folk arts, a project that has delighted and engrossed me ever since.

Next time I visited, my family asked about my trip. I launched eagerly into a description of the dramatic change in tone and quality of life when I crossed the Bulgarian border into Romania. Suddenly, my father interrupted. "Have you ever read Marx?" I was startled: "What?" "I said have you ever read Karl Marx?" I admitted I hadn't —not in any depth. I'd nearly forgotten those were "Marxist" countries. Somewhere there must have been a Karl Marx Square or Avenue, possibly a statue—it seemed to have little to do with the people I'd met. "Then what makes you think," he said, "you can go around telling everybody what's what in the communist countries? At least I've *read* Karl Marx!"

I found a good excuse to leave the room and went back to work translating the magnificent Romanian ballad, "Mioritsa." My father's arm was already in a sling; within two months, it would be gone, the first part to be buried. It was scarcely the time to have entered into competition with him (and surely I was not devoid of a triumphant pride in so doing); I hope I had not realized I might win. Besides, I had challenged at least two of the basic assumptions which supported his ego: first, that the Eastern Europeans were to be scorned, ignored, and kept poor; second, that the artist was to be scorned, ignored, and kept poor. Worst, I had achieved the independence he had so long verbally demanded but had actually thwarted. Not only was he losing the ability to help me, I would no longer need his help.

VI. GRANDFATHERS AND SONS

Only on my mother's side did I have a living great-grandparent. Summers, we would visit her family—my mother drove, alone with us children, from Pennsylvania to Kansas, a feat of which she was exceedingly proud. There, in the airy house of her father and step-mother, my great-grandfather, a dark, shriveled gnome, would occasionally stalk from his room to threaten us all with perdition. Otherwise, he read the Bible in his room all day. One afternoon as I sat at their dining room table assembling a model airplane, the old man suddenly appeared, glared at the pieces I had so meticulously glued together, then shook his cane at me and declaimed: "Works of the devil! Works of the devil!" he repeated, clumping back into his room.

It was whispered that the old man had worked at least one of his eleven sons to death in the field. I attribute this story more to well-earned malice against him than to accurate diagnosis. Such things did not seem possible if you looked at another of his sons— my grandfather. He was well over six feet, healthy and powerful-looking with a ruddy visage, a big, grizzled man with shaggy black eyebrows. His daily life cannot have been easy: his household included not only his senile father but also a daughter by his second wife, a lifelong invalid who could voice only vague noises and had to be carried from bed to the toilet many times a day. Yet every day he bustled cheerfully about his tasks: chopping firewood, wringing the necks of chickens, heaving the long handle over a steaming, sudsy tub of a manual washing machine.

Unlike his father, a farmer and part-time preacher, he was a full-time minister; he signed letters not with his name, Will Murchie, but with a Biblical citation, "Phil. IV, 4." One of the favorite family stories told how, when younger, he would sit composing sermons while my mother or her older sister clambered over him as over some friendly but preoccupied mountain. One day, a lady from his congregation knocked at the door and got a start when he, leaving his desk, appeared before her unaware that my mother had put his hair into braids and ribbons.

I never saw him read a Bible or write a sermon; by then, I suppose, he had much by heart. An officer of the church synod, he put much of his time into physically dismantling churches, loading them on boxcars, then reconstructing them where they were needed. Once, having completed such a relocation, he had found the beauty of his handiwork marred by a surrounding field of dead grass. Wanting the church to look its best for its opening the next Sunday, he set fire to the grass and burned down the church he had just moved and reerected. This proved not so unfortunate: the insurance paid for an entire new church. Hearing this story for the first time, I had wisecracked, "They may get you for arson, Parson"—one of my first efforts at either rhyme or wit, and deservedly one of the least warmly received.

Much as I admired my grandfather, I was shocked by a vigor that seemed at such variance with anything I'd known. I could not imagine wringing a chicken's neck, let alone holding its head while its body scuttled about the yard. When he touched me after scooping a dead grasshopper from the rain barrel, I squealed and backed away blamefully. Still, neither my suspicion that so much vitality must be improper nor his disapproval of my smart-alecky rhyme and squeamishness soured our relationship.

I heard him preach only once; I was disappointed. Often, though, he took me along to the auction house where we joined a jollier congregation listening to the chant and blarney of the shirtsleeved auctioneer who was, he told me, a scoundrel but of whom he was obviously fond. I have never lost a taste for old furniture, a hankering to peer into boxes marked VARIOUS, to snoop into what other people have lived with. If my poetry readings sound like a cross between a Protestant sermon and a country auctioneer's chant, that is no accident. When, at the age of sixty, I finally got an auctioneer's spiel into a poem, I felt I had achieved at least one part of my calling.

On my father's side, my paternal grandfather was a much-loved family doctor. Our town was full of crusty and eccentric physicians: Dr. Louden who looked like a Welsh magician, older than stones; "Hing" Carter who, seeing a certain young spark drive a fancy team and surrey through town, had snorted, "Kid gloves and no socks!"; and Dr. Benson who asked about his patients' symptoms, then reached deep into his pocket, pulled out a handful of pills, blew away the tobacco dust and commanded, "Take two white ones now, two red ones every morning, and a green one every night." This outraged the town: he cured everything. My grandfather was known for other qualities—above all, reliability and charity. To have such qualities noised about can cost you. Many of my grandfather's patients did not pay him—many *could* not.

He had earlier been a surgeon. Then a kerosene heater had exploded; he had gone back into the house for his children and severely burned his hands. Unfit for surgery, he became a general practitioner. He never spoke of this, but my parents said it was the great sorrow of his life. The scar tissue on his hands never looked all that bad to me. He was still pretty deft when the need arose: one day, well before my time, his younger son, Stew, burst into his office, gasping and choking. The children had been sticking beans or stones in their noses; one had lodged in the boy's windpipe. My grandfather, who'd been paring his nails, wiped the pocketknife on his trousers, dipped it in alcohol, set his fingers on his son's throat and did a swift tracheotomy, folding a piece of heavy paper into the slit to hold it open till they arrived at the hospital. Seeing the neat white scar on my uncle's throat, I often thought my grandfather might have kept his career. Still, though this might have brought him prestige and money, he could never have achieved the prestige he held in our town. When he died, the headline was as huge and black as for the declaration, a year or two later, of World War II.

There often arises, in our family politics, an alliance between children and grandparents against the common enemy. Grandparents are often less stern than parents, though in my case quite the opposite was true. Nonetheless, I had, at least for a time, a closer affinity with my grandfather than with my father. He fussed over the grandbabies, naming their fingers in an old Scottish game:

> Meentie-meentie,
> Podie-podie,
> Laddy wastell,
> Lady finger, . . .

GREAT ODD-A-MON-DOD!!!

This was delivered in a heavy Scottish burr; only after a long pause was the final, awe-inspiring name uttered in sonorous growls with much ferocious shaking of the thumb in question. This always produced gales of laughter from the so-inventoried child. He called me his "braw digne wastell," though my father could have warned him that I was neither brave nor a warrior. Our town had no auction; instead, when the circus or a carnival came, my grandfather would take me down early in the morning "to pay our respects to The Elephant." (The daredevil performers sometimes came to him for drugs without which they dared not perform; I think he usually refused.) Or I would go with him on house calls. He had a Model A Ford that, once I was perched on the front seat, he would crank by hand, then come around to climb in behind the steering wheel. Between us sat the satchel with his stethoscope and long black leather case of pill bottles—I still see such cases, sometimes, in antique shops. Occasionally there was a box of groceries for some family in unusually dire straits or to whom he felt specially close.

We bumped over potholed roads to farmhouses in the country-side or to the poorer parts of town where millworkers and common laborers lived. The country was in the depths of the Depression: mills were faltering, strikes and violence were common. President Hoover had promised that no one would starve, yet there were beggars downtown, tramps came daily for handouts, children sold doilies their mothers had crocheted, and in winter some of the homeless were allowed to spend nights in the city jail. One day, a butter truck lost its brakes on a steep hill leading into town; in no time families were out scraping butter off the rock wall where the truck had crashed. They did try to avoid any that was marked by blood or hair.

This grandfather, like my mother's father, was a large man though neither so tall nor so trim. He had a large scrofulous-looking nose and tended to portliness—at family dinners, he, his two sons and his son-in-law held meat- and fat-eating contests. I've seen him fork up a piece of sizzling beef fat, too hot to touch, and pop it in his mouth to the disgust and envy of the whole table. Otherwise, he sat

quietly in idle moments, his heavy, scarred hands folded in his lap,
or holding a tiny volume of Bobby Burns. His father had come over
from Scotland and had named him Bruce; when he read Burns
aloud, he affected a slight burr. Sometimes he would sing Burns's
songs or the old ballads:

> Come down, come down, Lady Margaret, he cried,
> Come down and kiss me fairly
> Or I swear by the brand that I hold in my hand
> I will not leave a standing stane in Airlie.

or:

> Scots, wha hae wi' Wallace bled,
> Scots, wham Bruce has aften led,
> Welcome to your gory bed
> Or to victorie!

I little guessed I would come to love and sing those songs
myself. I confess a preference for "Edward," "The Gairdener Child,"
or "The Baron o' Brackley," and am less taken by Burns's own
poems than by his song collections, especially the bawdy songs he
gathered and published in Bowdlerized versions, so saving them
from extinction. Only when I was over thirty-five and twice married
did my family think me old enough to know that, like Herrick,
Burns was a distant forebear—but not by marriage. They wanted to
protect me from that knowledge, I suppose, but like a recessive gene
or a tendency to theft, those songs and poems were deep in the
grain. Or perhaps I simply took the infection from my grandfather.

Even more ominously, my grandfather wrote short stories in
his spare moments. After he died, my father showed me some of
them. One told about two young boys who lived in a poverty-
stricken backwoods area but had saved up a few pennies to buy a
sack of ginger snaps. Through some misfortune, of course, they lost
both their money and the cookies. I suppose this tale was modeled
on those of Ernest Thompson Seton, whose *Two Little Savages* I had
read religiously. I fantasized myself one of its heroes, two farm boys

who take Indian names and live, part-time, out in the woods. I think he introduced me to that book—he certainly introduced me to the woods.

Several times, he took me to camp out in the "Hogback," a wooded area in northern Pennsylvania where he had grown up. On the edge of a meadow, we pitched a lean-to against his car, set up canvas cots, and built a campfire. He talked about his early life there and of the small game he had then killed for the family table. Once he had shot a squirrel which, when he picked it up, sank both front teeth clean through his finger and hung on, whirling through the air as he did a vigorous dance never before seen in that part of the country. We had brought along his revolver and saw many squirrels but, whatever his reason, he never fired it.

On a side trip, we visited my hermit uncle, Albert Herrick, who lived in a tiny cabin—filled, it was rumored, with herbs which he dried and sold to druggists. Beside this cabin stood a towering elm to which he carried thirty buckets of water every day. The spring being half a mile away, he walked, in his old age, fifteen miles a day for his tree. A prissy child, I saw my tiny wrist pass into his massive ham of a fist, then felt ashamed when it came back soiled. Back in the Hogback, we hunted up Lizzie Royer, an aged crone who owned a tin shack on the far side of a swinging cable footbridge, and wore a dress made of flour sacks and high black Keds like the poor children at school. I thought she, like the old hag in Seton's book, could have scratched and lit a match on the bare side of her leg.

Though I wondered at these independent souls, I was still a pampered and pettish child. Chilly on my bare cot under the little awning-tent my grandfather had attached to the side of his Ford coupe, my complaints kept us both awake all night. When we went fishing, I was too finicky to put a worm on the hook, too fussy to eat the fish we caught. The breaking point of our relation came some years later and concerned my sister Barbara, whom he called "Tappy" for "Tadpole." He became angry about something I had said or done to her and with the way my parents, especially my mother, spoiled me. I, in turn, as fond of undeserved advantage as most, took offence and, with my mother's tacit blessing, started to avoid him.

Though I did not return to the Hogback, the boys my age hiked out, from time to time, to Brady's Run, a large forested area about five miles from my home. I sometimes went and talked with Old Jack, yet another hermit, a strangely literate and well-educated man who had a rough hut there. I loved the woods, yet something—no doubt my mother's silent disapproval and my corresponding timidity—kept me home, inside the house most of the time. My grandfather had by then recognized that, far from being a "braw digne wastell," I was even less the boy of his imagination than was his own son, my father.

Still, my grandfather surely left traces. Not only in those songs and ballads, in the simple fact of being a writer, but also in my desire for a countrified and isolated existence, for a house in the woods. Nothing of the sort could be found in my father's life. He had rebelled against his father; rebelling against him in turn, I came back to his father. I may owe my grandfather, too, some of my fascination with foreign folkways and ethnic arts. He took me to Scotch Picnics in Pittsburgh to hear the skirl of pipes, watch the caber toss, see the Highland Fling and Sword Dances. As an adult I went more often to the celebration of Greeks, Romanians, Ukrainians—the "foreigners" his Wasp wife and children looked down on. He, too, sometimes talked them down, as was expected of a pillar of society. Still, he had real contact with them as fellow mortals. Besides, the Scotland we talked about, that he sang about, was as mythical to us (and to him) as Transylvania or Pago Pago. The songs and dances which we thought part of our heritage and birthright were ultimately alien and exotic. If I see more czardases and syrtos than Highland dances, hear more bouzoukis and cembalons than bagpipes, I probably do so companioned by his memory.

And I must admit that Scottish bagpipes stand my hair highest; all my life they have continued to reappear and haunt me. Every few years, when I was a boy, a bagpipe band—in full Highland military regalia, kilts, sporrans, plaids, the pipes squealing and howling, the muckle drummer wearing a leopard skin and twirling his drumsticks high overhead, the stately drum major striding ahead with his five-foot baton (not like the trivial shiny rods that nubile American girls spin, those erotic propellers, but rather an awesome mace and instrument of office)—sprang up on the edge of our city. How it got there, I never knew—there were no other towns out that way for it to come *from*. At a slow march, it made its way through the main street of town: through Morado, past the tube mill into College Hill, then down past the College and the cork works, through the residential areas into the business section, downhill again into another, poorer area where mill workers, mostly central Europeans or Blacks, lived and finally across the Beaver River Bridge to New Brighton, our neighbor city and deadly rival.

On down through the industrial towns, one after another, it passed—New Brighton, Rochester, Ambridge, Sewickley—toward Pittsburgh. Behind them, as in a scene from some vernacular *Carmen*, came an enormous crowd of kids, marching, mimicking, laughing, chattering. If they had meant to take us on some new and fatal Children's Crusade, or like Browning's vengeful piper, march us all into the blank earth of some hillside, we would have gone. But no, they merely marched ahead. Finally, some five or six towns downriver—by then the broader Ohio River—we would phone our parents to come and get us; most of us hadn't even taken time to pick up change so we could catch a bus home.

It happened to me again as an adult. In the Navy's Yeoman School at Bainbridge, Maryland, just as we were emerging from the showers after a long day of classes, calisthenics and marching, marching, marching, we had mail call. Once, someone in the next barracks received—in the mail!—a full set of pipes. We heard him outside setting the drones, then fingering the chanter and suddenly we dropped what we were doing—dropped what we had thought to be the most precious objects in life: letters from home, letters from girls—and were following him down the barracks road clad in shower clogs, socks, boots with no socks, bare feet, towels, skivvies, smuggled bathrobes, undershorts. After a full day of marching we had loathed, we were marching again—for fun! We marched defiantly, not into the cannon's mouth, but into the teeth of military authority. Consider the penalties: in a training camp, you are permitted only what you hate; if you start liking anything, that automatically places it "off limits." Yet, who can resist a bagpipe?

If I do derive such fascinations from my grandfather, my father seemed to inherit chiefly his weakness before his wife. My grandmother, born Mae Fogel, was a genteel, fussy lady, frail and willowy, probably attractive when young. She disapproved of much about my grandfather and did not hesitate to impose her values. Inside her house, which his long hours supported and from whose burning he had saved their children, he could not smoke except in his office. As for that office, she would not let him have it decorated in the white and sanitary style which was coming into fashion and was soon demanded. This hurt his practice. It was further damaged when she began to take over his waiting room, filling it with hirsute and venomous-looking plants which hung down like omnivorous vines. She herself began to preempt this as her sitting room where she would chat with, and pass judgment upon, his waiting patients. She was right: he lost money by keeping patients who could not pay. Her efforts to screen his waiting room, however, also discouraged many of the well-to-do and respectable to whose care she felt he should confine himself.

What troubles had passed between my father and his own, I never learned, beyond the uproar caused by my father's choice of a Midwestern wife and his defection to accountancy. As I've noted, his family eventually forgave him—especially since, during the economy's near-collapse, he became its most prosperous member. As he remarked, you can neither stay in business nor go out of it without an accountant. Once, deep in the Depression, my father unexpectedly met his employer, a Mr. D. G. Sisterson, while both were on business trips to New York. Having run short of cash, he asked if his boss could spare a small loan. "Sure," was the reply as the older man reached into an upper left-hand vest pocket, "do you want it in fifties," and simultaneously into a lower right-hand vest pocket, "or hundreds?"

Eventually, having his own business, my father employed not only his younger brother, Stew, and my two sisters, but also my younger sister's husband, who in time filled in for my defection and took over the business. Indeed, when my grandfather's generosity, bad choices in the market, and my grandmother's willfulness combined to put them in financial difficulties, my father had helped them out. He came to terms with them (my mother forgave them just as little as she forgave anyone else) and they with him, through the kindly offices of need.

Very late in my father's life, a few days after he and I had clashed as to who better understood the Balkans, we had another talk. When I mentioned that I was having trouble sleeping, he offered me some sleeping pills—the same pills, I thought, which he had saved against the onset of just such a terminal illness. I had not expected that generosity; it would not have been right to ask whether, in his condition—his arm in a sling, the probability of metastasis very high—he should spare the pills; I accepted. To my further surprise, he slipped his hand out of the sling, selected one from among the dozens of plastic medicine bottles on the table beside him (only a few contained sleeping pills) and poured out several capsules into a separate bottle for me.

In that moment, my father took on, I think, the doctor's role he had once refused and, so doing, made me his agent toward his own father. Can he have suspected all along that it was he and not myself who resembled Bazarov—the rebellious, nihilistic son who, on the verge, himself, of annihilation, was reconciled to and joined in the medical practice of his father, the old village doctor who had loved him almost to dotage. Grappling a pen in his fingers, already blue and swollen, he wrote out—I came across that bottle again not too long ago—the completely unnecessary instructions: "Take one or two at bedtime."

I saw him only once after that. I was beginning to uncover some of the truth about my family and myself. Intolerant of the damage our lies had done, still shaken (as he was, too) by my sister's death, I could not bear to go back again and acquiesce in the lies he was erecting, like a hospital screen, around his dying.

I suppose I, too, may eventually need to make some such reconciliation with him, possibly through my children. I see no way yet that I could assume the role he urged upon me. I still hate chess, can play neither billiards nor baseball, cannot add two and two. My important personal and financial papers always get misplaced; I do not understand them and as a result (or is it the cause?) am terrified of them. The annual struggle with Internal Revenue forms induces such dread and despair that three wives in a row have taken over that job rather than live with me while *I* did it.

But I will not play the accountant for my children. You may infer, if you like, some similarity between an autobiographical sketch and a balance sheet. Even so, I will not get to total up and balance the liabilities and assets, the profits and losses, the health of the industry; that's done by outside auditors.

VII. LOVE AND/OR WAR

Why was our teacher crying—unashamedly, in front of us all? What should she care if we were finally in the war? Nobody thought fighting would come to this country, much less this town. If it lasted, *we* might have to go to it; she wouldn't. We were used to war talk; year after year, our home radios had talked about plebiscites, treaties, battles, countries fallen: other peoples' war. We had heard the voices of Mussolini, of Hitler. That morning, we'd all been herded into the school auditorium where a huge radio console had been rolled out to carry the voice of Franklin Delano Roosevelt saying that the Japanese had bombed Pearl Harbor. Could she be crying for *us*?

Year by year, while I finished high school and started college, that war became a little less of a rumor, more a living presence. We had blackouts, rationing, newsreels, patriotic songs on the radio. The war, like love, was on every public tongue; we were expected to have strong feelings—but *what* feelings? Men I knew got drafted; a neighbor who'd played in Uncle Stew's tennis club died in a training accident. A boy who had bullied me in the high school band dropped out of school to join the Marines; he was killed. I did not admit, even to myself, a feeling that this proved the world's, even God's, justice.

Our band director's name was Adolphe—Adolphe J. Pletincks, a drillmaster worthy of SS sergeancy, who wore, moreover, a tiny mustache not unlike Hitler's. He, though, was Italian and wore it to look like a nobler despot, Toscanini. Unceasingly he exhorted us that, because of "our boys overseas," we must march better, play better, win more competitions. To botch a maneuver during the football halftime would "let *them* down." Absurdly, this worked; we took every prize in the area.

I once knew a Russian who, during World War II, had served a prison sentence in Siberia—the best years of his life, he said: "free" men were in the army. The time I served in the tiny hyper-Christian college a block from my home could have been as luxuriously carnal if I'd had sense or nerve. We were strictly forbidden to smoke, drink, or dance, but a kindlier tolerance was turned toward couples who slipped off nightly to the "Big Rock" or the woods behind the practice football field. Instead, I wrote a column in the campus paper, helped write a musical comedy, acted in plays and skits, was student conductor of the chorus. The older girls, who would normally have scorned freshmen, sought us out, praised our performances, took us to necking parties.

So love and war, or sex and war, arrived in tandem; at times they seemed equally daunting. When, at earlier parties, our high school gang had played Spin-the-Bottle or Post Office, I abstained—though I had a heavy crush on one of the girls, a slender blond, outside whose house I paced longingly late at night, whistling sad songs. Still earlier, I had taken another girl, as pretty but less fashionable, to a barn party. I think she liked me; in time she became a dancer, shared my love of music, and proved superbly sexual with one of my friends. Alas, while other couples kept disappearing into the hay mow, I not only failed to vanish *with* her, I vanished *from* her, seeking noisier sports among the boys. Later, at school functions, I seldom danced with girls, getting instead into athletic jitterbug contests with other boys—much as young Hungarians and Romanians display *for* their girls rather than dance *with* them. By the time I finished high school, though, the drives grew stronger, even if my nerves did not. The few times I'd tried to kiss a girl, I had shivered so heavily that I had to plead a sudden chill and hurry home. In college, I did manage to try a little petting with the older girls, though even then I was known to deliver to a partner impromptu sermonettes on the subject of French kissing.

Meantime, I'd been attracted to a girl in my freshman class, a minister's daughter whose name, Amber, recalled the heroine of a then-scandalous novel. She agreed, after our first movie or pizza, to drive out somewhere and park; I tried not to betray that I had no idea where one *could*. As soon as I kissed her she began to moan and tremble, fumbling at my clothes. I backed out of our woodland cranny in such panic that I stuck the car in a ditch—embarrassing, but at least a crisis I could manage.

Another night, we went to lie in the tall grass behind the practice field; again I fled. Despite my best sermonettes, passion still shook her even more wildly than fear shook me. One day, when she'd quite justly fled to her room in the girls' dorm, I got the nerve to follow upstairs, risking expulsion. I dared climb or enter little else. Already weary, no doubt, of her father's sermons on love and sex, she had no need of mine and soon moved on to a college air cadet.

Still, the draft loomed closer. I felt unable to face that war without someone to be in love with, someone to come back to—a feeling shared, oddly enough, by most young men. And I soon met another girl who fit, more or less, the romantic ideal of the moment: slender, blond, and rather timid both sexually and personally. We started dating and soon decided we were in the grip of a great passion. We did feel *something* powerful, wanted to call it love and to believe that, since it would surely last forever, you could mitigate your death or build your life around it.

Getting drafted must be much like what a frog feels, being taken into a larger organization—say, a heron. Instantly, you become one in a line of naked men, examined, poked at, numbered, rushed from place to place, questioned, insulted, shouted at, given indecipherable but inexorable commands. Then, strange clothes are hurled at you and you emerge, as from a new, more fearful birth trauma, into an area of barracks and asphalt-covered, phlegm-splattered drill yards. I have no way to convey how utterly you become nobody, vulnerable, almost transparent. The world's center of gravity has shifted, never again fully aligned with yourself.

In school, I had been one of the best students, and one of the class clowns—a role self-deprecating enough to make me almost acceptable to tougher, less studious classmates. In the Navy, nothing I did, said, or could think up was funny. Music was no help; after boot camp, I kept a few scores with me but how many sailors care about Palestrina? Actually, a man two bunks away *did* care, but he'd been second organist at St. Patrick's in New York and found my learning not exactly impressive. At base after base I joined the Bluejackets' Choir hoping to find a berth as music specialist; I found, instead, others better prepared, more experienced. I had no idea how to relate to the men around me or how to restore any trace of existence to what had once seemed the plain facts of life.

Randall Jarrell ended a fine little poem, "Mail Call," by saying "the soldier simply wishes for his name"—if called, it will bring him a letter and prove possible, possibly even recoverable, the person he had been. The surest proof came in love letters. Mail call was the best, or worst, moment of each day; you approached carefully any man whose name had not been called. Only a "Dear John" letter was worse—we felt, mawkishly no doubt, that with no one to come back to, a man was less likely to come back. As if wanting something more intensely could make it more likely to happen!

Evenings, when others read, played cards, went to the canteen, I stayed in the barracks to write my family or my girl. I was determined to write her every night; once or twice, I refused to leave the base on liberty lest I miss a day. My friends—eventually I had some—were aghast. Though I had little to say beyond the tritest lovers' formulae from movies or the radio, my letters grew longer and longer. I cultivated outsized handwriting to eat up more space on the page, making it all bulkier, more substantial.

No doubt I hoped—in vain—to coerce more and longer answers, more impassioned declarations. How else could I impress my less romantic, less sublimated mates? My best friend at several successive camps, known as "J.C.," got letters from *his* girl signed, "Again, Johnny! Again!" Chastity had to go far to match that! J.C.'s cynical cockiness often shocked me. When an older platoon member and former lay preacher, Charles Birdey, returned from liberty full of oily self-praise for the weekend spent comforting his impoverished grandmother, J.C. shouted across the barracks, "Hey, Birdey, did you get in her pants?"

I was shocked, too, when friends, whose wives' or girlfriends' fidelity was so crucial to them, felt no constancy incumbent on themselves. Of course, we demand more of others' morals, especially of those we love, than of our own; then, too, men were expected to be sexually freer. And the fact of facing possible death or injury made many feel driven to, and justified in, sexual inconstancies. To me, all premarital sex was immoral; when I did not dare have sex with my own girlfriend, I could scarcely imagine it with anyone else. That seemed as preposterous to my friends as their attitudes seemed scandalous to me.

Still, some of my notions *were* changing. Home for ten days leave after boot camp, I became more urgent and our love play more intense. I wonder what I'd have done if she *had* been willing. She wasn't. And partly because of that—what might now seem a strong deterrent—we got engaged.

At the same time, I found myself—to my surprise—darkly resentful against my parents, as if they had somehow caused the war. It might have made some sense to feel that our lifestyle had been one, at least, of the war's causes. Or that my upbringing had left me woefully ill-equipped for the world I faced. What I *did* feel was the spoiled child's sense that its parents, the gods of his tiny cosmos, were to blame for all trials or dangers. My feelings about God, the one in church, were as yet unchanged.

Other attitudes did change: I was finding that, in real need or trouble, if help came it was seldom from the appointed or promised channels. In boot camp, my greatest fear had been of the "swimming lessons"; I could swim a little but had always dreaded the water. Those "lessons" consisted of ordering a shivering clump of thirty or forty naked men to jump, all in one herd, into the pool—then strike out, arms thrashing, bodies thumping and jostling, for the far end. For our last lesson, we had to step off a high wooden tower, plunging into the water feet first. In the chow hall, the night before that test, I went to pieces, hysterical.

A boy my own age—vulgar, irreverent, a loudmouth I'd never willingly have spoken to—took me in hand. "You come right beside me," he said. "We'll go off together; it's a snap." When we'd climbed the platform atop the tower, he stepped out, whooping, comically kicking and flailing; then I, too, stepped into the air. Falling for what seemed hours, I heard a small, regretful voice I've heard again several times when I thought my life about to end in a car crash or a fall, saying with stupid sincerity: "Oh, I wish I was back up there." Then I was in the water, splashing toward the edge. Climbing out, I saw three or four men still standing at one side of the tower; until and unless they jumped, they would not go home on leave. As for the boy who led me through, I think I barely thanked him, if even that.

Meantime, neither engagement nor sexual fidelity forbade me the meaner betrayals of courtship and mating. In San Francisco, waiting to be shipped out, I went one night to a USO dance where I met, and seemed more or less acceptable to, a group of girls who came there regularly. One who seemed to like me—whom I would now think very handsome, with strawberry blond hair coiled in a high informal hairdo and long gold ear-pendants her family had brought from Hungary—invited me to spend the night at her mother's apartment. I was doubly disturbed: first, I was attracted to a second girl, more glamorous and surrounded by other sailors; second, I feared the invitation might be immoral in intent. I was mistaken. The day before we shipped out I repaid her kindness by phoning and tricking her out of the address of the other girl. No doubt she saw through my duplicity but gave me the address anyway. I must have thought such manipulations less culpable than simply having sex with someone you had not married.

We all imagined that, once our troopship left San Francisco, we would enter a world of combat and physical violence; for most, this was not true. We also imagined we were leaving the world of sex; this was equally false—we were only entering its darker hemisphere.

One can't ask much of a troopship. The USS *General Collins* held some 5,000 enlisted men, sailors and Marines, crammed into its holds. There, we lay in six-high bunks so narrow that, to turn over, you usually had to crawl out first. Once in, you were buffeted if the man below you shifted his weight, got stepped on if someone above climbed out. Except for the few hours we were allowed on deck, there was no place else but the aisles, already full of bulky green seabags and other gear, men sharpening knives, playing cards, comparing photos.

There *were* a few saltwater showers in the head, but these did little good—perhaps you were cleaner; you felt even stickier. Back in the hold, you had no room to unpack a seabag and find fresher clothes. In the head, the long, deep urinal troughs plugged up and filled with dark yellow or milky orange slosh that, as we got into higher seas, splashed onto the floor and anyone around. No one reported this for fear of being appointed to correct it. Meantime, the food was poor and we, with seasickness and no exercise, handled it poorly; diarrhea was general. The reek of urine, of sweat and vomit, of sour digestions, the smell of fear, grew.

Most of the day, most of the night, you lay awake hearing the curses, farts, the groans and shouts of those who *could* sleep through the deafening creak of the ship's incessant roll and lurch. We knew that such "Liberty Ships," as their maker Henry Kaiser called them, sometimes split apart in heavy seas. And we *had* enemies. Entering your compartment, you passed through heavy bulkhead doors with long-handled clamps, called "dogs," on both sides. In a troopship's hold, these handles appeared only on the outside; if our hold took a torpedo, that bulkhead would be "dogged down" from the outside, sealing us in to drown—so possibly saving the ship.

It was preached to us, again and again, that there were no atheists in foxholes. I never dug a foxhole, never saw a hostile Japanese soldier, sailor, ship, or plane. Still, in wartime, a ship at sea is always in some peril. We never knew, when our convoy fired its heavy guns, dropped depth charges, whether Japanese ships might be approaching, submarines prowling. A vision of 5,000 men in the water, wounded, burned and burning, crawling, clawing, fighting and drowning each other for some piece of floating gear, would not leave my mind.

The voices of all past authorities—parents, teachers, preachers—counseled me to pray. That's just what I'd done all through my childhood and teens. Obsessed with religion, convinced my every motion was watched by some higher, probably disapproving, power, I had never so much as shot a basketball, answered a teacher's question, or hurled a stone at a tree without a silent prayer. My playmates who wondered why I did most of those things so poorly, sometimes asked why my lips were always moving; I had ignored the questions.

The same authorities would have given the same advice now. Yet every man on every ship that had ever gone down had been praying to one God or another; they had still drowned. What use was praying? Having a god? Who could believe that our convoy, sweating, cursing, crawling across the Pacific toward the terrors of hand-to-hand combat, was controlled by anything but human greed and stupidity? To think that any god—much less a God simultaneously all-knowing, all-powerful and all-good—could create or direct such atrocities seemed imbecilic and blasphemous at once. No doubt the intensity of my former beliefs now contributed to their evaporation. The atheism of J.C. and my other well-read friends claimed me for good. Later, timidity or practical concerns might urge the self-deceit that I was agnostic; that lie never lasted long.

In harbor at Hawaii, we anchored near the burned-out hulk of the USS *Arizona*, still on its side where the bombs had left it when all this began. It was even stranger to stand for hours in sweat-soaked fatigues, lined up at the ship's rail staring at palm trees, beach cabanas, surfboards, luxury hotels—a land we, like Moses, were permitted to see but not enter.

At sea again, even more painfully tantalizing was the vision of another life on the upper decks and off limits to us. There, the officers and nurses—who had gone ashore at Hawaii—lounged, ate and drank, played games, sunbathed. Possibly unaware of conditions below decks, they flaunted their luxury, comfort, and freedom. Nurses and Wave officers, in bathing suits, leaned at the railings, displaying themselves above men already half-crazed with sex. Those men filled with a seething rage, not only for the officers they already resented, but for these women—who were known, behind their backs, only as "cunts." Such rage was in part planned from still higher authority and was intended, part of the systematic stripping away of one's sense of personal worth or selfhood, so that resulting rages might be turned against an enemy. We learned, soon enough, how savagely this could backfire.

When our small group of yeomen—clerical workers—disembarked at Saipan in the Marianas, just one week after the last Japanese bombing there, no one knew what outfit we belonged to. We moved into an empty barracks and were free to roam the island; many set out at once for souvenirs. Up the hillside behind our barracks, half-hidden in jungle growth, were caves where fighting had gone on. There I found several of our outfit hauling out cases of Japanese grenades and mortar shells which they, blankly ignorant of munitions, were dismantling. Farther down the hillside, a man I knew was wrenching the leg off a Japanese corpse; a closer friend knocked the teeth out of a Japanese skull to wear on his key ring.

If such acts were meant to demonstrate fearlessness, we fooled no one. Japanese soldiers still roamed the hills, hiding from our

Marines who made occasional sorties to slaughter them—some under orders, some for sport. On our first day, Willy Gunn, who had grown up near the original Tobacco Road, had a starved-out face and a high, whiny voice, came racing into the barracks, puffing and panting, holding his chest and gasping, "I just seen a Jap! I just seen a Jap!" J.C. shouted, "What'd ya do, Willy? Didja run?" "Hell, no," he wheezed. "But I sure passed six men that *did*!"

Months later, we located those ledges and land spits at the water's edge where Japanese women had sat, hours, holding their children, before resolving to walk on out into the ocean. We never found the cave that we'd heard had held the naked and unmarked bodies of a Japanese man and woman killed by concussion in the act of making love. I think we might have felt it a sort of shrine, but would, no doubt, have had to desecrate it.

In any case, and probably just as well for us, our holiday ended; we were assigned to the Receiving Ship. Our main task would be to arrange transportation for men assigned to other bases or ships. Though we, too, were advanced base personnel—"dusty sailors"— our offices were actually aboard a small ship, the USS *Spark*, an LST which had cracked up in each of four invasions, had a split hull and had been beached to keep it from sinking. Our "transients"— survivors of ships lost in naval battles, men who'd been left ashore for medical or other reasons, new draftees going to their first assignments—slept in the tank deck on folding cots under bright lights and the never-ending roar of pumps that kept only half that deck dry. Days, we tried to keep them all on "working parties"— mostly busy work which they diligently shirked—chipping and painting the ruined ship. I was supposedly in charge of these transients, most of whom outranked me so I ended up doing the larger part of the work. Everything about the ship had a bad name with the Naval Base on the beach. Our Executive Officer, a Regular Navy ensign, had been assigned to us as an informal punishment after he'd been caught making love on the beach with actress-comedienne Betty Hutton when her USO show had earlier visited the island.

We soon heard that another USO troop had its own misadventures on Saipan. Late one night after the show, some SPs from the

Naval Base, trying to trace a stolen jeep, inadvertently discovered that the showgirls had taken over some abandoned Marine barracks in the hills as an impromptu brothel. Long lines of soldiers, sailors, and Marines stretched into the jungle. Since most of us wouldn't have lasted more than seconds, the lines moved briskly; at $100 a trick (easily equal to $1,000 now), the take must have been impressive. Meantime, their male manager was discovered on the beach with an officer, also male. All this had to be hushed up, of course, and the troupe rushed off the island—on to the next engagement where, no doubt, similar opportunities would abound.

Recently, a friend told me that this event is reported to have happened on most of the Pacific bases and may well be a legend. Thinking back, there *had* been a USO troop on the island that night, but I find little further evidence. Perhaps the real point is that such was our condition, our hopes and suspicions, that we *could* believe the story on no more evidence. There was no question that some enlisted men later found our Executive Officer again on the beach—this time with a nurse. Both went to the hospital; she was raped, his shoulder broken. After the taunting provocation we'd seen aboard ship, it was hard to feel as indignant as one should. But everyone was repelled when the bodies of another officer and nurse were found there with more than twenty-five submachine-gun slugs apiece. We were relieved by that gang's arrest and execution, yet I never felt quite the fury toward them that I did against such novels and plays as *Mr. Roberts* or *South Pacific*—works for which the American public paid generously to lie about their men and women at war. I could not fully enjoy the chorus of enlisted men peeking into the nurses' shower, singing jocularly that "There is nothing like a dame," or the genitally nominated Nelly Forbush singing that she was "gonna wash that man right outta [her] hair."

I knew of only one other execution on that island—that of a medical corpsman who hadn't realized that it was wood, not grain, alcohol he was selling from the sick bay. Several men died, others went blind; he was hanged. Much later, our office had a Regular Navy Chief Yeoman—Sammy, an older man, thin and wiry. He'd grown up, he told us in his sharp Appalachian accent, in West Virginia where his brother ran a whorehouse. He found, he said, that he could lay seven girls a night—if they were seven different girls. One Christmas Eve he brought us some Cokes and a bottle of sick-bay alcohol he'd either bought or stolen. None of us—eighteen- and nineteen-year-old draftees—dared touch it. Only months before, alone in that office one night, I had drunk my first can of beer. For hours, I had shaken with a dread of eternal damnation quite beyond anything the most impassioned young woman could have induced. It had not occurred to me that atheists should not fear damnation.

The only comparable dread I can recall had struck me on another Christmas Eve in my early teens. For some time, during extended baths, I had been making private investigations related to my advancing puberty. On that evening, quite suddenly, the bathtub, the bathroom, my whole corner of the cosmos, was filled with electricity; gross physical changes occurred. God and my grandfather, who had recently died, must have seen it all. To go straight from that supposedly cleansing bath to receive lavish and expensive Christmas gifts made me only the more surely damned. Of course I had not suspended investigations; neither did I now stop drinking beer. Sammy's alcohol, though, might not only damn, but could blind or kill you. We knew he had risked the brig or prison to please us at Christmas and were grateful; his disgust for such pantywaists was immitigable.

The brig, strangely enough, was attached to the Receiving Ship and during my first months, until a clerical job opened up, I was a brig guard. This seemed the most direct of many ironies. One morning while we had still been in training near San Francisco, a hand-to-hand combat instructor had given fifty or sixty of us a lesson in how, if caught without any weapons, you could blind a man with your bare hands, then rip off most of his face. Perhaps no one actually expected us to do that; this could have been a test of our willingness to surrender former beliefs and feelings. In any case, I believed they meant me to do that. It seemed no less clear that *any* man deserved a better death and that I had no business receiving such instructions or putting myself where I might commit such acts—as, indeed, I knew I might if my life were at stake. It was only many years later, falling apart in a psychiatrist's office, that I was able to recover that scene—but I knew that morning that I could go on only because of cowardice at the thought of opposing my society. It was still theoretically possible then to declare oneself a conscientious objector, but my loss of religious beliefs soon afterward left only one alternative—prison.

Lacking the nerve for prison, I became a brig guard. Every morning, wearing clean blue dungarees and a bright white cap, a .45 strapped to my belt, I brought out onto the deck a line of prisoners, mostly Blacks who were in for such minor infractions as gambling, fighting, unauthorized absences, or were waiting trial on more serious charges. All wore filthy green fatigues tied together with bits of string; their low overseas boots flapped, comically, as they shambled along the deck—belts and shoelaces were forbidden for fear they might strangle someone or hang themselves in the brig. When everyone else had gone through the chow line, they ate, then were assigned to daylong tasks. Back in the brig at night, they were assigned to six-high bunks in a cramped compartment with one barred porthole for ventilation and a bucket in the corner for a toilet.

Among our prisoners was a medical corpsman, a Southerner, one of our few whites. When I asked why he was there, I thought he said, "Raping the goats," but later realized he'd said "Gooks," meaning the Chamorro women, native to the island, who were either patients or workers in the hospital ashore. "There was no rape to it," he said, "they wanted it as much as I did." Still, the Navy had decided that nonwhites were, like girls under sixteen, incapable of consent; he would stand trial, face probable conviction, prison and a ruined life. Among his keepers, though, was a brig guard, named Chuck Kroll, who not only admitted but bragged about raping at gunpoint a British girl who'd gone out but wouldn't lay with him.

And, as we've since heard about most American prisons, if women were unknown in the brig, sex and rape were not. Masturbation must have been constant. Bobby Cotton, whose shuffle and evasiveness were much like the wily Black actor of stage and screen, once told the head guard, "You tell ol' man Keene I beat my meat. I'll get me a BCD; I'll get me out of here!" When the guard reported this to amuse the captain, Keene retorted, "You tell Cotton I beat *my* meat and I hope he enjoys it as much as I do."

Two sailors were brought aboard by the SPs one night, to be charged in the morning with drunkenness. For some reason they were not put in with the other prisoners, but alone in a small, irregularly shaped compartment with no porthole—a "sweat box" reserved for men in solitary or given special punishments. When, as night guard, I made my regular check, the smaller, younger man begged to be brought out. Alone, he said the other man had chased him all over that little box, trying to overpower and rape him. I put him back just long enough to verify this, then handcuffed the older, surlier one to a central beam and left both for the night. I found myself shocked not only at the drunken sailor's brutality, but also at my response. Though we went on using this box for solitary confinement, it was dangerous to leave anyone immobilized in so hot and confined a space. Still, nothing serious had happened and we made jokes about the smaller man's plight.

No one was much amused when, some weeks later, another new prisoner *was* put in with the regulars for the night. When the substitute guard, Polidori—I was off duty—looked in around 6 AM, the new prisoner claimed he had been gang-raped (in Navy lingo, "pogued" or "cornholed") repeatedly during the night. All guards converged on the brig at once, carrying Thompson submachine guns, bringing the prisoners up to the captain's cabin where each, one by one, was questioned. Many admitted having anal intercourse with the new prisoner; all claimed he had been willing, had even offered himself. That question was never settled, but to the Navy this made no difference; our prisoners faced long sentences in full-scale Naval prisons. There might also be nasty problems for us and for our officers, since it became clear that the brig had gone unchecked most of the night.

The captain's solution was to impose punishment there on the *Spark*—in pretended mercy bringing no charges, effectively covering up from the Base authorities what had happened. Any prisoner clearly involved was put on heavy labor for two weeks. They spent their nights in a larger sweatbox, sleeping in their work clothes on the steel deck under bright lights. For the first two nights, Polidori was kept there with them—till it became clear his life was in danger.

As the days wore on, these prisoners grew wearier, more harried; rage and tension grew. Every night, every hour on the hour, I would open my .45's holster flap, tie the loose end to my thigh, release the safety catch, then take a flashlight and go below. One of the dogs on the compartment's bulkhead door had been removed; I looked through this hole before entering. After the second night, there was always an open eye on the other side, looking back. Despite their supposed isolation, the prisoners had a contact outside and knew when I was coming. One by one, I pulled the remaining dogs, swung the heavy door open, ordered the man standing inside to step back, then went in between the two lines of men. I ordered any still lying down to get on their feet, brought them all to attention, dismissed them and left.

I still wonder where I found the nerve. I doubt that I was concerned with the justice or injustice of their case; I had no way to know who had consented to what. The sleaziness of our officers' reaction seemed to remove most moral questions. I must have feared the officers, authority in general, more than I feared the prisoners. They, in turn, knew I must obey orders or become a prisoner myself. Still, I was the one charged to torment them; one day, when I was surrounded by other prisoners, one accosted me.

"Heavy" Humbert, this Black giant, did not belong in the brig at all. In a fight over a poker game aboard an aircraft carrier, he had been hit in the back with a fire ax. After months in the hospital, he had testified against his attacker, then had been erroneously sent to our brig. The Navy, of course, would do nothing to correct this injustice, but most of us, knowing of it, gave him what consideration we could. He was gigantic, amiable, much liked. Now he loomed over me, furious. Their outside contact had told the prisoners that, the night before, I had once called them on the half, not the full, hour. They thought I'd waked them once too often. In fact, I'd called them once *less* than ordered. Either through fear, sympathy, or neglect, I had been half an hour late for one call, and continued after that on the half hours. That, of course, could have put me in trouble. Doubting that Heavy believed me, I sought the company of another guard. Surprisingly, I was less frightened of Heavy than sorry he thought I might enjoy tormenting him. True, it looked as if he had taken some pleasure in abusing the new prisoner. Yet again, he'd been mistreated by the Navy; he had little reason to trust anyone carrying out its orders.

Most of this improved, of course, once we moved ashore into the newly built barracks and Quonset offices of the Receiving Station. Some of our equipment, trucks and jeeps were returned to us; we had facilities and proper quarters for our transients. We were, moreover, adjacent to the main Naval Base and subject to its surveillance. The brig was turned over to the Base and run by Marine guards—far more brutal, efficient, and orderly than we had been. The *Spark,* newly chipped and painted from bow to stern, was towed into Tanapag Harbor, filled with cement, then sunk to help build up the reef.

On shore, we went on shipping men to battles and invasions where many would be killed or maimed. The only Japanese we saw were former soldiers who slipped down out of the hills, passing for Chamorros or for the Koreans they had once brought there as slave labor but who now worked for the U.S. From time to time, the man ahead of, or behind, you in the chow line would suddenly gasp, then break for the jungle. You had been standing beside your recent enemy, a Japanese soldier, now completely helpless—starving but afraid to surrender.

The violent air and nightmare sexuality of the *Spark* gradually faded into the past. In our barracks, a tall, well-built and quiet boy named, ironically, Manley, fell hopelessly for the boy in the next bunk—a cocky street-type named Marcio. Manley followed this ugly, small thug everywhere, ran his errands, did his laundry. I could never have expected my macho friends' reaction: they shared my surprise that Manley had been drawn to Marcio, rather than the other way around. And no one mocked them—not even behind their backs. It had been so long since we had seen genuine affection that we watched with something close to awe.

Eventually, the atom bomb ended the fighting, the Marshall Plan was announced as a humanitarian project toward a brighter future; just one day later it was revealed as a weapon in the new war already begun. What had been masked as concern for the hungry and homeless proved merely a willingness to starve out any who did not vote our way, would not make themselves our market. I think I have never felt a more basic betrayal.

Some months later, a friend in our office told me he was going to slip his papers in with those of the next group going back for discharge. Neither of us was due for several months, but he said our new Ensign never read what he was signing; once we were back, they'd have to discharge us. I typed up my own papers and we inserted both in the pile. Next morning, we were on the dock with our gear, part of another slow-moving line of men. When our Ensign passed, he peered at us, puzzled, but said nothing. We climbed the long gangplank, unable to believe it had worked. In weeks we passed through San Francisco again, then the long train ride home, and we were out. On our own.

Jarrell once told me that when the Air Force asked for slogans which might move men to fight better, he had offered: "We're fighting so the whole world won't be like the Army." He seemed genuinely surprised his motto hadn't been chosen. The Navy, for all its rules and regulations, had at times felt curiously free. True, you had to get up at a certain time, eat at assigned places and times, dress in an assigned manner, work assigned hours at assigned jobs. Then, though, you were free for things you hadn't been at home. Oddly enough, all those assignments freed you from having to find any worthy purpose or course for your life—even if you'd found such a thing, you'd not have been permitted to follow it.

But above all, and especially overseas, you were free to think and feel whatever you thought and felt—to question your religious beliefs or your country's motives. For the moment, your doubts could not affect the greedy and ruthless forces moving that country relentlessly against other greedy and ruthless forces. On the island, everyone I talked to had known, precisely and unhesitatingly, the mercantile causes behind our war. By the time we reached San Francisco, they remembered none of it, returning to beliefs that coincided with American propaganda. As we sailed under the Golden Gate Bridge, its great vertical bars passing, first, over our heads, then behind our backs, Alcatraz to one side grotesquely abloom with lavender flowers, I had the sensation of passing from one kind of prison to another, one perhaps more pervasive and no less threatening.

Meantime, my feelings about my family had been undergoing similar, but slower, changes. I no longer felt so childishly blameful but, bit by bit, my sense of their reasonability and unquestioned moral rightness was profoundly weakened—by life under other regimes, by comparison with other families. In San Francisco, with J.C. and other friends, I had eaten rare steaks, drunk red wine; in the dining car crossing the continent, we had shrimp and fresh tomato quarters. I knew I'd never find such blessings in my parents' house. Those things, of course, were only symbols, but I would soon face the value systems for which they stood. In time, I came to feel grateful to the Navy, even to the war; no lesser force could have loosed me from my mother's will to spiritual dominion or from my ingrained dependence on her—though that liberation would still take years.

I had come back lacking religious faith, belief in my nation's benign mission, trust in my parents' sane "rightness," or in my own courage and secure purpose. The church had been right about one thing: its view of romantic love as competition to their form of faith. As soon as I gave up the notion that we lived in a world created for some "good" purpose by a Being in some way similar to a human soul, my need for such love seemed devouring. More than ever, I needed to convince myself that there was someone who loved me as much as I did, and that this would be the one enduring thing in a world where all would perish, a world unconcerned and senseless.

What my girl and I had felt so strongly before I went overseas, what we called love, should have been called terror. It was that which made us clutch at such frail reeds as one another—each depending, expecting, demanding that the other take the place of an orderly, benign universe dedicated to our comfort in daily life, our significant career, our cosmic centrality. And to that end, despite our own misgivings and our parents' protests, we threw ourselves around each other's necks like exhausted survivors of a sinking ship; we got married.

In our terror, our flight from freedom, we were much like that society which had helped form and define our hungers—a society with all the world before it, if not to command, at least to influence and help shape. Surely no such opportunity was ever offered any other nation. Daring neither total domination nor real freedom for others (meaning freedom *from* us), its moment of glory passed swifter than any in history. We were as much at the mercy of our greeds and fears as were those we'd fought and beaten.

As for me, I had managed to face the most horrifying of wars but quailed before the freedom to choose my own way of life. Within months I was again dependent on my family and, worse, on my young, timid wife. If belief in romantic love had survived my other faiths, marriage (just as my skeptical Navy friends had warned) would surely do away with that.

VIII. A LIBERAL EDUCATION: MENTORS, FOMENTERS, AND TORMENTORS

BACK TO SCHOOL

Most everyone agrees that the time just after World War II, when the colleges were full of GI bill veterans, was the Golden Age—or Golden Instant—of American education. Still, there were times when, with its overcrowded classes, long lines registering in field houses, married students living in barracks and Quonset areas, it seemed much like being back in the service. It, too, could lead you into harm's way.

Once out of the Navy, I decided I'd have to get out of music; I simply hadn't done the groundwork necessary by the time you're twenty. I felt, though, that I belonged somewhere in the arts and decided—on the absurd grounds that I had the basics: the English language—to try playwriting. I had seen somewhere—*Life* magazine?—an article about Paul Engle's writing workshops at the University of Iowa. I soon found, though, that playwriting was taught only in the theater; I had to persuade someone there to take me into their course. Sadly, I succeeded. The Theatre was in the hands of an aged tyrant named Edward Maybee, a crude and bullying businessman-type who had championed a costly new theater building with advanced stage machinery and elaborate equipment. This "ideal" physical plant, with its demands for popular and financial success, had quickly driven artistic life out of that once vital program.

My playwriting class was taught by a woman who'd been a classmate there of Tennessee Williams—whose first version of *A Glass Menagerie* had been rejected as a Master's thesis. Already stung by its success on Broadway, she called him a one-shot writer; then, months before the class I took, *A Streetcar Named Desire* had opened. Known generally as "The Bitch"—language not then used on campuses—she was absurdly rumored to be the model for Blanche DuBois.

From the first, she and I were at war. The first law of her formula for plays was that the leading character must be likable. I raised the spectres of Macbeth and Medea; she retorted that you had to learn the rules before you could break them. She paraded my first scenario—based on Trevor-Roper's *The Last Days of Hitler*—through the classroom between pinched fingers like a dead rat's tail while holding her nose with the other hand.

She proposed that, as a class, we jointly compose a scenario according to her formula. She picked the central character and situation: a young girl in an orphanage who dreams of becoming a concert pianist. Her mentor, the kindly headmistress, knows that the girl cannot succeed and wants to teach her a digitally related but humbler skill, typing. The required obstacle is that the girl has reached the age of graduation and the antagonist, head of the board of directors, is determined she must be ejected on schedule into a hostile world. Need I dredge up any more?

A first draft completed, she asked each of us, in turn, for criticism. Each declared it excellent—some remarked on the economy of cast and settings; one thought it might do a year in New York, then have a profitable run in little theaters. When she got to me— having sedulously avoided my help in the "communal" composition—I collected my nerve and said I thought it gawdawful. I probably played some variations on this theme. After class, one of the others—all theater majors—pulled me aside: "You idiot!—that play is in her doctoral dissertation!" They had all known.

Still, my own plays were terrible; only my teacher's doctrines could have made them worse. I wandered back into the Creative Writing Department and soon was sitting with, though not signed up for, the Poetry Workshop. I had no intention of writing poetry, but there, at least, I felt I might learn something about one of the arts. The students were extraordinarily gifted, some doing exciting work. Better, I could admire my teachers: they cared about their subject; they *knew* something about it.

I was terrified and exhilarated at once. I had never even heard of New Criticism or of T. S. Eliot. I suddenly realized that, through-out my two years at a small Covenanter college, I had taken A's in every course without understanding a word. I hadn't even known there was something you *could* understand. For two years, I read as if possessed; I was too scared to say Word One.

Among the workshop students was a gruff, bearlike veteran named Hood Gardner, several years older, silent, glowering, obviously respected by the others. Earlier, in the Art Department under Maricio Lasansky, he'd made some beautiful copper engravings; before that, he'd designed a striking lamp for an industrial design class, then a new typeface for a typography class. All he did bristled with invention; now he was in the fiction workshop writing a muscular novella. Almost at once, I attached myself to him.

One noon, I followed him to the barracks apartment where he lived with his wife and baby son; I couldn't have been more awestruck by a shah's palace. On the wall was one of his copper engravings; near it, his own map of the tiny Pacific island where he'd been stationed—a map accepted by the National Geographic Society; opposite, a rack of primitive spears and arrows his native workers had given him. The phonograph was playing a Violin Concerto by Delius, of whom I'd never heard. Hood sat, solid as a magistrate, in a gnarled diamond willow chair or would hold his naked baby son by both hands, dunking him in the kitchen sink, while we talked about Sartre—just then appearing in English and a heavy influence on Hood's novella. Hearing that the brightest of the student writers and intellectuals met at Hood's Quonset almost every night, I vowed to beat down the door if necessary.

Again, I was both terrified and exhilarated; my wife, Lila, was only terrified. Most veterans' wives worked: Hood's wife, Betty, was a clerk at the Psychiatric Hospital; Lila taught primary grades in a small town nearby. Leaving the Gardners' after our first evening there, she started to weep hysterically: "We must never, never go back there. Never. I feel so stupid, so ignorant. I know they're all making fun of me." In the small college we'd both attended, she'd been bored half frantic by her education classes; now she wanted to flee from anything livelier. I felt equally ignorant—but how else to correct that? Persuaded, finally, to return, she grew at ease, was liked and accepted. After several semesters as a listener, I was admitted to the poetry workshop. I'd found something I might be able to do.

Both fiction and poetry workshops were directed by Paul Engle—who, though he'd not founded them, was largely responsible for their success. It had once been expected he'd become a fine, perhaps a great, poet; this had not occurred. A fellow student once said that if Paul had a choice between two ways to do a thing—a simple, straightforward way and a complicated, difficult, underhanded way that was nearly as effective—he would always take the latter. A related predilection, I think, ruined his writing—again and again, a poem would broach a real and moving subject only to collapse into sentimentality or hot air. That same predilection, however, made him a superb administrator. And it may be that any such large and expensive program needs a person similarly gifted at its head.

Engle could be—and on occasion was—a brilliant teacher. He led us into the French Symbolists, Baudelaire and Verlaine, then did close analyses of Rimbaud's "Le Bateau Ivre" and the magnificent "Memoire." Multiple corridors, landscapes of expression opened, ways of meaning I had never imagined. Later, knowing Engle had lived in Germany, I brought him the Rückert texts set by Gustav Mahler as *Die Kindentotenlieder* and which I wanted to translate. Sensitively and precisely, he pinpointed the strengths and subtleties of those poems. Yet, if I'd presented those as my own poems, he'd have thought them sentimental or overemotional.

The problem lay, I think, in his own writing's history. Coming from a small town in Iowa, he'd been celebrated, when young, for long-lined, loose poems of a sort wrongly called Whitmanesque. Later, these had been attacked by the New Critics and writers influenced by the Symbolists, Pound and Eliot. Now he was championing those very writers who had savaged his early work. This might bespeak a willingness to see that one's opponents were right—perhaps, though, only that they were stronger. In any case, converts are liable to be stringent and dogmatic. Ignoring the real causes of his early work's artistic failure (an emotional and intellectual dishonesty that had also insured its popular success), he was obsessed with symptoms.

There were other problems—not least, that he was seldom present. He traveled about the country, later the world, spotting with great accuracy promising young poets and luring them to Iowa City. With missionary zeal he badgered administrators, legislators, businessmen for the funds to support those students, their courses, the writers who taught them. Even when in Iowa City, his mind was usually taken up with such problems; criticism of student work reverted to a sort of knee-jerk New Criticism. It is the classical dilemma of American education: those of highest ability don't want to administer; those of lesser ability are bound to administer for lesser purpose.

And deeper problems. Engle enlisted many students who had more promise, were on the verge of more achievement, than his own. That must have been hard to live with. He was. Subtle and energetic, he held the purse strings for graduate students—as the young mens' wives were supporting them, there were ready ways to destabilize their psyches. It was common to be invited to Engle's country house, a rundown estate in Stone City, for a party—then be asked to cut down some small trees on the grounds, to mow the lawn, to do other menial tasks. People moved to Iowa City, perhaps with families, on the promise of grants or fellowships which never materialized. "On-going" fellowships might suddenly be canceled. Once, Engle had appeared oblivious to a growing attraction between his appealing but fiercely neurotic wife and one of the graduate students, but then had walked in on an embarrassing, if not quite actionable, scene. I suppose all creative programs must have some students whose work is blocked; too many of ours had exceptional gifts but were unable, for long periods, to produce anything. True, those students often contributed greatly to others' work through generous criticism, but their own work and careers faltered. Surely part of this lay in their relations with the director.

I suppose someone might claim this could have served as preparation for the academic and literary worlds we would soon enter. Once, at a party given for Robert Penn Warren, Paul shocked everyone by telling his recurrent nightmare. He was a prisoner, he said, in a concentration camp where he'd been singled out for a specially degrading punishment. Along the camp's outer rock wall, about six feet off the ground, was a series of holes or depressions. Brought out naked before the massed prisoners, he had to bend over and grasp his ankles, then, hoisted by the guards, insert his feet into two of the depressions. The guards and prisoners jeering at him, he must then draw out one foot at a time, moving it to the next hole and so proceeding around the wall like a fly. But, he said, after a while he found he could do this surprisingly well—better, in fact, than anyone had ever done it. Soon he was simply whizzing around the wall while guards and prisoners, no longer jeering, looked on with amazement and admiration.

We were astonished not only by the horrors of this dream but also by his recounting it at a party where many (Warren not least) would understand. If only his poems had offered such revelations! At parties, horrors were not scarce: one evening I was met at the door by Engle's wife who, though approaching derangement, still seemed appealing. "Well, Mary, how's it going?" I asked. "Oh, I don't know," she said in the hearing of everyone, "I love him but it's so awful!" After a pause, she went on, "I went over and had most of my plumbing out last week. He might as well have that, he's had all the rest." Such scenes moved us sometimes to sympathy for Engle, sometimes for her; we all knew sympathies could be dangerous.

For years, Engle was very generous toward me; then, without informing me, he suddenly cut off my fellowship. I had recently been divorced and had support payments to meet; this could have put me in serious trouble. Fortunately, Rhodes Dunlap, a Renaissance scholar, warned me then added me to *his* list. When I had so many to feel grateful toward—such scholars as Dunlap, Victor Harris, and John McGalliard, not to mention, for the moment, my writing teachers—it was sad to leave with bitter feelings toward the very person who had, chiefly, made the experience possible. I think it fair to note, though, that my feelings were reciprocated. When I attended a reunion some years later, Paul, as master of ceremonies over a vast luncheon, was able to recognize and introduce to the group every other person in the room—industrialists, legislators, teachers, former students. There was a gratifying wave of laughter when he had to ask who I was.

THE BIG BOYS

Engle's absences had one splendid side effect: substitutes. Ruthven Todd, the Scottish poet, came during my first year, though I only got to know him later; freed from his rocky upland farm in Scotland, he seldom left his stool in a local bar. Later, there were Reed Whittemore, Karl Shapiro, Robert Lowell, John Berryman— besides those who came for shorter periods: Warren, Brooks, Tate, Ransom, Ciardi, Dylan Thomas, Jarrell.

When I first heard Lowell was coming, I scarcely dared believe it. Soon after going to Iowa, I had fallen in love with the poetry of William Empson, author of *Seven Types of Ambiguity* and of intensely ambiguous, highly intellectual poems. Having written several villanelles imitating Empson's, I then moved on to Lowell. His early poems—*Lord Weary's Castle* had just won the Pulitzer Prize— overwhelmed young readers, much as Swinburne's had an earlier generation in England. I cannot say we understood them. I cannot say I understand them now—or even that Lowell understood them. But, after the dry, etiolated language and attitudes of Eliot, we were ravenous for their vigor. A Lowell poem seemed like some massive generator, steel-jacketed in formal metrics against the throb of rhetoric and imagery. Even before we'd heard he was coming, I'd been writing like him.

Until his arrival, he was the one topic of conversation: the time he had done as a conscientious objector, his periods of madness, his past violence. We were surprised to find that, though tall and powerfully built, he seemed the gentlest of mortals, clumsily anxious to please. Talking to you, he'd lean one cheek on his fist, or rest his chin on the back of one straightened hand; the elbow purportedly supporting that hand and head often rested on empty air. Meantime, his free hand, its wrist cramped at a sharp angle, the first two fingers pointing, made jabs and slashes in the air. This broken wrist—often associated with weakness or effeminacy—seemed here to betoken almost an excess of force, leashed-in but undiminished.

Lowell's massive, unwieldy appearance seemed an objective correlative to his mind and personality. Almost devoid of graceful expression, he often broached an opinion or subject in the most jolting and awkward manner—sometimes he seemed simply off the track. Soon, though, the mass and power of that mind overbore doubts or objections. You could never predict his opinion, what associations he might draw, toward any subject. That, of course, may almost be a definition of brilliance—that it throws out unexpectable ideas. Yet this was so marked in Lowell that I sometimes wondered if he did not, like certain British writers I've known, deliberately make outlandish comments either to spark conversation or to appear clever. Surely a sort of aggression was embodied here—on a level, though, that provoked not mere controversy but real thought.

However high the expectations, almost no one was disappointed by Lowell's teaching—it was only years later, from comments published in *The Gettysburg Review*, that I learned of Philip Levine's resentment. Lowell came, one semester each, for several years and usually taught at least one course in masterpieces of English poetry. For each session he picked a poet or even a single poem, then for several hours would free-associate to that work. Wyatt, Raleigh, Milton's "Lycidas," Landor, Tennyson's "Tithonus"—week after week we came away staggered under a bombardment of ideas, ideas, ideas. None of those works would ever look the same; neither would our estimation of an adequate response to the work of art.

His workshops were, if anything, even more powerful. When Lowell "did" your poem, said one student, it was as if a muscle-bound octopus came and sat down on it. Then, deliberately, it would stretch out one tentacle and haul in Mythology, a second for Sociology, a third for Classical Literature, others for Religion, History, Psychology. Meantime, you sat there thinking, "This man *is* as mad as they said. None of this has anything to do with my poor little poem!" Then he began tying these disciplines, one by one, into your text; you saw that it DID have to do, had almost everything to do, with your poem.

My friend neglected to say that two days later you would run into Lowell on the street and he'd say, hunching over you with a concerned smile, "I've been thinking about that poem of yours— you know, the one with the rather grand language." (This was not a compliment.) "And I was all wrong about it. Now, what it's really about is . . ." He was off again, hauling you with him through new galaxies of idea and association. Who could feel less than grateful for a mind so massive, so unpredictable, so concerned?

No less exciting was the Greek Poetry Workshop—taught jointly by Lowell and Gerald Else, then the leading American classicist. The students were poets from the Workshop; none of the others had studied Greek. (I had taken beginning Greek twice and Homer once, but none of that had taken.) We moved through the *Iliad* at exactly six lines per meeting, taking apart every sentence, every word, to identify its root, the nature of any suffixes and prefixes, additions, eccentricities of Attic or Ionic speech, departures from normal syntax or usage. This two-hour class followed an unvarying format: for the first hour, Lowell went through our six lines throwing out incredibly provocative, far-reaching theories about their meaning and implications; for the second hour, Else went through the same lines telling what they *really* meant. The class seemed almost a liberal education in itself; even Else said that doing the *Iliad* so slowly taught him things he'd never noticed.

The incredible force and extension of Lowell's mind seemed to me frighteningly involved with his extreme personality changes, his manic-depressive episodes. Little by little, month by month, the reach and power diminished, area after area of that mind was sealed off. Finally only a weary, gray shadow remained. Then, as that dammed-up force began to reassert itself, he might grow fiercely destructive to himself and others.

In his work, Lowell intimates that, if his wives were hectoring or slighting to him, that recalled his earlier situation with his mother; he felt this to be the nature of affection. Once, in some conversation, I started, "Oh, marriage is always . . ." He, no doubt dreading my impending truism, concluded, ". . . a rat-fight." When he could endure his situation and its concomitant depression no longer, he usually got a new girlfriend and broke into manic violence. I knew he could not have been easy to live with, that he had chosen and contributed to his situation, yet that made it no less painful to observe. I still felt something approaching awe for him and found it hard to feel friendly to anyone less deferential to him.

Fortunately, he had no violent episodes at Iowa; I was never present when he did. There, I met his wife, Elizabeth Hardwick, only briefly. She was apparently ill quite often; sometimes, after he had talked with some of us downstairs, or brought us home from some party, a group of friends might be received in her bedroom. Usually languid and exhausted, she once or twice became so excited at the mention of an absent acquaintance that she would get out of bed to "do" them. These imitations were exquisite, crackling with energy, but you never wanted to leave the room for long.

In time, I came to be one of the senior workshop members; my work was liked by Lowell and others—not merely, I think, because it resembled his. I did not care to recognize how exact, how exacting, that resemblance was, apparently content just to win a place among writers and teachers whom I revered.

Randall Jarrell, more than anyone, helped jolt me into other directions. I was able to study with him through the generosity of Catherine Drinker Bowen, the biographer, who'd given a lecture at Iowa City and then returned her fee, to be given to younger writers. This, plus a fellowship from the Rocky Mountain Writers' Conference, took me to Boulder, Colorado, that summer. Since the conference was to last only three weeks—most are even shorter—I expected little more than a respite from academia and a collapsing marriage.

I thought I had some notion of what to expect of Jarrell. Knowing he and Lowell were close, I assumed he would, in some way, resemble his ponderous friend. I knew Jarrell's poems, especially those about World War II, and thought him the only American poet serious enough to deal with that cataclysm. Expecting him to concur with other poets and critics who'd seen my work, I selected a sample, including pieces admired by Robert Penn Warren, Ransom, Brooks, and Tate. (It *did* seem odd that no two had liked the same poem!)

We met; I was flabbergasted. Slender and graceful, with a pencil-line mustache, he displayed the manners and vocabulary of a lively but spoiled little girl. "Gee," his voice skated to a high note as he lounged almost seductively against a stone wall, "don't you just love Colorado? I think Colorado's simply *dovey!*" If Lowell had come down on me like an avalanche, Jarrell came like an Alpine skier schussing across that broken surface and piping (as Lowell recounts in an actual memory of him), "I feel just like an angel!"

His classes were as startling. Instead of discussing our poems in class, he read and analyzed other poems, beginning with an hour-long exegesis of "Frankie and Johnny." This ballad, in Brooks and Warren's version, he thought one of the half-dozen best poems composed in America; after his explication, I could scarcely dissent. The next class session, we tackled "Prufrock." Once again he demonstrated that, even on this famous, much-belabored text, we simply had no idea what was going on. Neither had the critics and teachers we'd consulted. Hankering after big ideas and impressive terms, we'd thought the poem somehow depicted Eliot's movement toward religious belief; we had no inkling that the poem contains a lady or that Prufrock feels an urge to "go, through certain half-deserted streets," to her apartment where, despite the women who may "come and go" there, he will ask an "overwhelming question." Throughout, the poem's intent is to dissuade himself from any such hazard.

Most of the students were distressed that he discussed their work only in private. If I also was, I knew I'd been so enlightened that I could scarcely complain. Lowell's analyses had tended to the highly intellectual; Jarrell's, the emotional and personal. To my surprise, he cared about the exact dramatic scene and situation, about who was speaking and for what purpose. Could that be as important as grand ideas and terminology? Having nailed down these matters, Jarrell sensed, impeccably, what specific choices of language revealed about the speaker's character and emotions.

In "Frankie and Johnny"—which most teachers would have dismissed—we hadn't even realized that everyone except the judge is Black, that Frankie is a prostitute and Johnny her pimp (not pander), or that she finds him in bed with Alice Fry—wearing a Stetson she must have bought him. "Did you ever meet a man," Jarrell asked, "so happy-go-lucky that he might come to the dinner table with his hat on? Could you tell more about a man's character if you wrote a whole book about him?"

Again, discussing the details of clothing, Jarrell revealed more of Prufrock's character than most critics do in many volumes:

> My morning coat, my collar mounting firmly to the chin,
> My necktie rich and modest, but asserted by a simple pin—

It's as if, said Jarrell, the man had been born in a morning coat which he'd shed and grown anew every six months; as if a tortoise should confide, "I know I'm old and my neck is all wrinkled, but just look at my shell . . . my beautiful shell . . . my beautiful tortoiseshell shell!" Absurdly, it is Prufrock's collar (surely an old-fashioned, high, starched one) which he imagines "mounting firmly"—language suitable to Roland or Galahad before a bastion. Prufrock will mount firmly neither bastion, stairs, nor lady. Against the women who might mock his thin arms and legs, his thinning hair, he can marshal only the richness of his necktie, then having done so, must correct himself with the thought that "We rich people must be modest." Yet that must be balanced with, "But that's my problem: I'm too modest. I must be more assertive." Then, countering that, "But I simply can't stand assertive people!" So he must insert the "simple" pin—an adjective defining precisely what he is not!

Jarrell must have spent five minutes on those lines—every second of them revealing. He moved on to the climactic scene where the imagined lady will finally turn to Prufrock, throwing off her shawl to leave her arms open, her throat and shoulders bare, then—in the very epitome of cruelty—turn toward the window to dismiss him: "That is not what I meant. That is not it at all." We hadn't even known the poem had any such scene!

In private conferences, Jarrell was remarkably kind, I think, to most students' poems. He may have thought many students lacking in talent, so not worth troubling. He regarded highly the work of one man among the younger students and of one little old lady. Having lost her husband, this lady had taken a job as a government stenographer. Sent to Guam, she'd been assigned to record court-martials. What she'd seen there had been so cruelly unjust, so unjustifiable, that most of her beliefs had collapsed. Her poems were about those cases; Jarrell said one of them had moved him to tears. Meantime, the older participants (whose presence paid for the fellowships of younger students like myself) tried to coax her back into more comfortable acceptances. He always encouraged her work but knew, I think, that her age might make the loneliness of such knowledge unendurable.

His attitude toward my work was harsher and more public: "You're some good." He thought me nearly obliterated, though, by the influence of Tate, of other New Critics, most especially of Lowell. "Do you know, Snodgrass," he crowed, "you're writing the very best second-rate Lowell in the whole country? The trouble is there's only one person writing any first-rate Lowell: Lowell." Sitting on the patio, surrounded by tables of students with their Cokes and sandwiches, he would pick up one of my poems, loudly declaim a line or two, then slap his thigh, howling, "Snodgrass, you wrote that! You really did! That!" Or he would whoop, "What are you trying to do? Turn yourself into a fireworks factory?"

If Lowell had seemed like an octopus, Jarrell was like a dolphin, swiftly slicing curvets through the sea, uttering outrageous messages in almost supersonic squeaks, bumping sharks to death with his nose and, in a closed tank, liable to kill every other creature for the fun of it. I often thought that if the wit even of his everyday conversation hadn't kept me weak with laughter, I might have hit him.

In the sheaf I'd given him, he had liked only two poems—both translations. One was that passage where Ovid tells of Jupiter as a white bull carrying off Europa; the other, the first of Rilke's *Sonnets to Orpheus*. I'd done both pretty much as exercises—the Rilke because I'd seen a printed version so poor I thought I couldn't do worse. These made sense to him, he said; they embodied an emotion he could experience. I think it hadn't occurred to me that this counted. He thought my own poems academic exercises: they didn't, on the one hand, make much sense, or, on the other, have such magical language that you could get along without it.

Because of my Rilke translation and my poem called "Orpheus" (which was, he must have guessed, about my failing marriage), he sent me to look up Rilke's "Orpheus. Eurydice. Hermes." Unquestionably a masterpiece, it depicts, in nearly surreal images, Orpheus' fearful journey into the underworld, where he will sing to regain his wife. She, utterly changed by death, must be led by Hermes, the messenger god, following Orpheus' voice back to the upper world. As always, Orpheus, wracked by fears she may not be following, must not look back until they reach that realm. As always, just at the threshold, he turns. The god is horrified: "O but he is looking at us!" She, in response, speaks one syllable: "Wer?"—"Who?" It isn't that she hates you, Jarrell said; not that she is wicked; not that you are worthless. It is simply that she has no idea who you are, no idea you are even there. Can you do anything with fancy language, he asked, to match the sheer invention of that?—the utter bleakness? I began to see what he was getting at.

In a strange way, too, I may have affected Jarrell's life during that conference: I probably brought him together with his second wife. During registration, she had asked me who this Jarrell was; having signed up for a fiction workshop and children's writing, she wondered if she should take him also. I told her to drop everything else. She took him so completely that both almost disappeared from the conference. If you saw them at all, they were holding hands, cooing and ogling each other like adolescents as they sauntered away—evenings, to dance; daytimes, to his match with the local tennis pro. Someone who'd known him earlier, at Greensboro, said Jarrell and his first wife had been seen skipping across campus together, then cuddling in the back row of the movie, the day before their divorce proceedings began.

Despite all his brilliance, despite all I was learning, I could not always be sorry to lack Jarrell's company. On the opening day, I had noticed Jarrell's racket and asked if he'd like to play; he replied that he was very good and didn't like to play anyone who wasn't. I backed off, but later had a minor revenge at Ping-Pong. No, I didn't beat him, but I did scare him—I think I was the better player, but simply couldn't want to win any game that much. Again, at the end of the conference, the students did skits and songs and I got to "do" Jarrell. In time, I grew grateful to him: he'd been right; my poems improved.

Not, though, at once. Over several years, other pressures grew. My marriage fell apart and I had to take outside jobs to meet support payments. I was desperate at not being allowed to see my baby daughter. Partly because of the marital failure, partly because my writing was blocked, I went into therapy. There, I noticed that of the two of us, the doctor and myself, one sounded like a textbook; it wasn't him. Similarly, my poems weren't finding my own voice or any subject I really cared about. This recognition, together with Jarrell's criticism and the example of certain songs I was translating, led me to write markedly different poems, in particular the cycle of poems about my daughter which first brought me general notice.

At that time, strange to say, Engle and others in the workshop were more sympathetic to my new poems than was Lowell, who tried to dissuade me from this course. John Berryman, who came for one semester seemed, if not wildly enthusiastic, encouraging. Several lines, there, still contain revisions he suggested.

By that time, however, my life was in such turmoil that I saw rather little of Berryman. I was working, first, in a grubby small hotel, then at the Veterans' Hospital. My impression is that his classes were no less stimulating than either Lowell's or Jarrell's. He is harder, though, to sum up: not quite so ponderously intellectual as Lowell, nor as emotionally brilliant as Jarrell. Full, though, of startling insights. He took us through the ending of *A Winter's Tale* and selected passages of "Song of Myself." Reading the miraculous last section of the Whitman, he looked up and said, "You know what that proves? That proves most people can't write poetry."

Berryman's writing classes were specially valuable, partly because he made specific assignments to a roomful of already highly accomplished students. When they handed in their assignments one day, he sat a moment leafing through the papers, paused to look at one, then glared at the class. "It just is not right," he said, "to get a sonnet like *that* as a classroom assignment." He was looking at Donald Justice's poem "The Wall," telling how the angels, driving Adam and Eve from Paradise, raise above the closed gates their dazzling and fearful wings. Later, he assigned us to write a poem in stanzas about a death; I wrote "A Flat One" about a patient I had looked after at the Veterans' Hospital. I later had to comb Lowell's language out of this piece, as well as its Symbolist stasis, but felt grateful to Berryman for a poem it wouldn't have occurred to me to write.

He once said that the poet's career should consist of, first, finding who they were, finding their own voice. Then, though, they would have to set about finding their opposite—the thing and voice that they were not. Finally, they would have to make a synthesis of these oppositions. This had a relation—never an easy one—to his own career and his effect on students. He tended to jolt you out of any easy definition of yourself or your limits. The poem was for him, more than either Lowell or Jarrell, a leap into the unknown.

Meantime, his own career seemed stalled. Some time before, he had published *Homage to Mistress Bradstreet*, which won multiple awards and which many had proclaimed the great American long poem. By this time, they had stopped saying that. No one was reading his little pamphlet *His Thought Made Pockets and the Plane Buckt*, which contained a number of concentration camp poems and several sketches toward the loopy brilliance of his finest achievement—the *Dream Songs*. All the cockeyed fancydance and fireworks of those poems was now going into talk at cocktail parties, bars, all-night drinking sessions. If he didn't seem to be involved with any women just then, propositioned none of his students, he made up for that. Once he'd had a few drinks, you could not get away; if his monologues couldn't hold you, he would grab your arm or would sing—surely the worst singing I ever heard. Unlike the quiet little man who walked about campus wearing a porkpie hat, this Berryman was frightening; I started avoiding him. He got into a fight with his landlord, thence into jail and finally out of town with the semester unfinished. He was already well into the drunken wallow of his later years.

Other teachers I recall in scanter detail, some because my personal affairs became so embattled, some because they came for shorter periods, some because they were simply less memorable. Karl Shapiro took the workshop for a semester, but commuted from Chicago only one day a week. Considering his position as editor of *Poetry* and the rambunctious heresy of his recent critical dicta, we were astonished at how vague he seemed about student poems. He often brought along the magazine's coming issue and discussed its poems instead. Even here he was oddly noncommittal, almost evasive. We asked why he had picked this or that poem (the undertone of which always meant, "Why *that* instead of my poems that you praised but rejected last month?"). His answer usually ran more or less that, well, it's not very good but the writer did some fine poems fifteen years ago and people would want to know what he's up to lately. We couldn't figure out just what he liked or wanted; we wondered if *he* could.

Of those who came just for an evening's reading or lecture, then a workshop meeting, easily the most notable was Dylan Thomas, who came twice. We had the usual longed-for scandals: the stevedore's language, the crush on a dumpy local waitress, the Tournament of Insults at the chairman's party. One year, having fallen in with truck drivers, he rolled off the train dead-drunk to announce, "This is the night I don't go on!" He was rushed to the writers' Quonset office where the bathroom had an actual tub, dunked in icy water, rushed back into his clothes and brought to the Old Capital's Senate Chamber, where he gave one of his most beautiful readings. Before and between poems, his speech was slurred, shambling, obscene; suddenly, for the poem, he would shift into that sonorous, nearly Shakespearean voice still so familiar on recordings. The effect was so electrifying that one couldn't help wonder how much it might be calculated. The audience—many of whom had admired Eliot's dry and weary renderings—was forced into difficult reappraisals.

His meetings with the workshop, like Shapiro's, passed over the students' poems; he read, marvelously, his favorites—Hardy's "Ah, Are You Digging on My Grave," Hodgson's "Eve," suggestive limericks, Ransom's "Captain Carpenter." At less disastrous parties he retold the myths of his own malfeasances—e.g., about the well-meaning London landlady who, not realizing he could only stomach a glass of milk and one of beer in the morning, brought him breakfasts of eggs and sausage, bacon, lox, ham. When every drawer in his rented room was filled with decaying delicacies, he'd had to move out. Alas, my only direct contact was to point him once toward the Men's Room.

The others who came for such short periods were frequently New Critics—Brooks, Tate, Warren, Ransom. As they were also Southern Agrarians, dialect problems sometimes developed. Warren, moreover, paced and mumbled. Tirelessly, he would stalk back and forth across the platform muttering enigmatically, then turn suddenly to declare "*And!*" Then he'd turn his back again, pace off several more stage lengths, whirling again to exclaim, "Theahfoah," or "Lak a ploohm!"

Ransom, the sweetest and courtliest of Southern Gentlemen, perhaps of mortals, once announced that he'd prepared an essay for us but didn't like it and would, instead, tell us about the "dipodics" which his friend, Harold Whitehall, had just declared to be the basis of much poetry. All our learned scholars sat transfixed, watching in awe and perplexity, their heads pivoting in unison from left to right to left to right again as if at some very slow Ping-Pong match. Before them, Ransom, with a conductor's follow-the-bouncing-ball gestures, recited:

"The NOATH wind doth BLOW
and WE shall have SNOW
And WHAT will the ROBin
do THEN . . ."

"Now you see," he explained, "theah's somethin' missin' theah; it wasn't enough. So they had to add somethin':
"pooah THING!"

On the stairway, leaving another occasion when he *had* read his prepared lecture, I heard a senior Professor ask a colleague, "What's this new critical term he's invented? Metapause—what does that mean? Metapause!"

All eccentricities and even extremities of opinion aside, these critics and writers all brought an air of intelligence, seriousness, commitment to and concern for literature. One never doubted—as so often since—that one belonged to a genuine university community, a body of scholars, critics, and writers who, even when dead wrong, truly cared about their subject.

Only one visitor brought a sense of emptiness and intellectual posturing—John Ciardi. His own poems, when he read them, seemed null or pretentious. Yet, because of his translation of Dante—surprisingly tone-deaf but still daring to use appropriate low-down language in *The Inferno*—one still had hopes for his workshop. He began by remarking that as poetry editor of *The Saturday Review of Literature* he received hundreds, even thousands of poems weekly; as soon as a poem lost his interest, he stopped reading. When he taught, he drew, instead, a blue line across the page at the point he would have stopped if not paid to continue. This already seemed questionable practice on several scores, but we held our peace. He turned to one of the student poems—a piece by Bill Stafford about how cedar trees manage to cling to even the rockiest, steepest cliffs in spite of high winds and pounding salt spray. "On this one," he said, "I'd have stopped right there where it says that whenever you come to such and such type of ocean cliff, 'as like as not, you'll find a cedar'. . ." What was wrong with that, we asked. "Why, that says 'as like as not'—that means 50 percent of the time. I've been on lots of beaches and cliffsides; you don't find cedars anything like 50 percent of the time." We protested that the phrase surely meant "often," but also some suggestion of admiration for the tree's toughness and tenacity. He replied, "But that's the point: you've got to say what you mean."

"I ran into a case like this the other day. One of my students was writing a story—he'd been a Marine in the war—about a troopship he'd been on. He had a phrase, 'When we arrived in mid-ocean . . .' I tried to explain that you just couldn't say that." By then we had broken into clamor. He went on, "You can't 'arrive' in mid-ocean. 'Arrive' comes from the Latin, *'ripa'* or 'bank'; *'Ad ripum'*—'to the bank or shore.' There's no bank or shore in mid-ocean! But you couldn't explain that to him—he was a Marine!"

I'd never before wanted to defend an American Marine. But none of us did—we had sunk into disbelief that we'd heard correctly. He continued, "Now look at this poem by Robert Frost— 'Mending Wall.' It starts, 'Something there is that doesn't love a wall, . . .'" The example proved *our* point, not his, but no one wanted to argue it. Better just get away as quickly and politely as possible.

CONTINUING EDUCATION

Of course, I encountered most of my teachers again. I cannot say many of them came to good ends. My best friend at Iowa, Hood Gardner, who'd taught me at least as much as any of the faculty, lost his first teaching job, came back to the University, changed fields several more times, and ended up making detailed medical drawings for the University hospitals. His son, a paratrooper, was killed in Vietnam. Hood and Betty broke up; he remarried. When I revisited Iowa City to give a reading, he seemed downcast and bitter. Even so, when he died unexpectedly, he remained a demigod for those close to him. My own daughter, who was raised there, said that his second wife and stepdaughter often picnicked beside his grave, where they had installed a tube in the ground and dropped sandwiches down for him.

I ran into Ciardi in Detroit at parties given by Charles Feinberg, a wealthy oil executive who collected manuscripts. I was not surprised to hear Feinberg relate that Ciardi had decided to become the first rich American poet. Not only was his deep voice to be heard over National Public Radio but, on the side, he sold real estate.

I reencountered Shapiro when I read at Nebraska, where he taught. I was much concerned at that time with the problems of raising children, and we shortly got into a heated argument on the subject. Shapiro declared that one should raise a child "like a sexual weed," giving them all freedoms they demanded so that they might grow up fully vital and sexually fulfilled. I suspected this would have precisely the opposite effect, abandoning them to the scant mercy of terrifying energies and drives. At the dinner table, his sullen but flirtatious teenaged daughter kept throwing pieces of meat from her plate at me.

As we started to leave for my reading, he appeared wearing a flamboyant shirt that provoked an outburst of scolding from his wife. Smiling—apparently having provoked the desired reaction—he slunk off to change. After the reading, we had just arrived at the chairman's party when he and his wife said they'd have to rush me away—their daughter had been at a dance and she might bring the boys home with her. In part, I was relieved to find how little his passionately argued convictions affected his conduct. That also made it clearer how he'd passed through so many allegiances: dedicated Jew, converted Catholic, Communist, academic Beatnik, conventional prosodist, etc.

For a long time I avoided Lowell—partly to keep my language and poetic practice free of his. Also, conversely, because he had written me that he was taking my poems about my daughter—which might never have been published without his support—as a model for his own work. I found this, in one I had nearly worshiped and whose style had so dominated me, hard to live with. I even became afraid—perhaps mistakenly, though not without evidence—that he might be influenced by some of the more destructive elements of my own life and behavior. When I did visit, Hardwick and I became steadily less friendly. If I did not see him during any actual breakdown, I did just before and shortly after; the change was appalling.

Once, I visited his class at Boston University. I couldn't believe how dull he appeared; the class was dreadful. I struggled to inject some life into the class, but my deference to him, my unfamiliarity with the students' work, my shock at his state—all conspired against that. As we left the building, he hovered over me much as before, saying, "I always feel you should be as numb as possible in class—not say too much that's interesting. You ought to give the students a chance—not just obliterate them."

During that same weekend, though, we had one splendid evening: in his study we stayed up working on his translation of Rilke's "Orpheus. Eurydice. Hermes"—the same poem Jarrell had shown me years before. At the time Lowell was influenced by the late poems of Ford Maddox Ford—which he'd been reading for me during the day—and was moving on from the *Life Studies* poems toward an even prosier style. I was astonished both at the flatness and slang of his renderings and at the liberties he took with the original. I've never held a brief for literal translation, but it hadn't occurred to me that you might take the original simply as a spring-board into a related, but different, poem. Jarrell had once said, about his own splendid translations, "I would never try to second-guess Rilke!" I had agreed. Now I had to rethink my position: after all, what was good enough for Wyatt in his versions of Petrarch just might be good enough for us.

If my poems had once pushed Lowell toward a simpler surface, he had now moved into areas of language I wouldn't have dared. For instance, in that poem's ending:

> Far there, dark against the clear entrance,
> stood some one, or rather no one
> you'd ever know. He stood and stared
> at the one level, inevitable road,
> as the reproachful god of messengers
> looking round, pushed off again.
> His caduceus was like a shotgun on his shoulder.

I recall that I had qualms about "no one / you'd ever know," which now seems, however un-Rilkean, brilliant. I still don't know what to think of that shotgun in the last line. In any case, though I'm glad there are more literal versions, I still see no reason to regret the existence of Lowell's.

We must have worked for three or four hours, until around 2 AM when Stanley Kunitz came in. Kunitz, usually unfriendly to me (and whose opinions I often thought mawkish), now worked over the same poem with Lowell while I took a lesser role. I was surprised by the quality and cogency of Kunitz's practical criticism. I came away drained but exhilarated; someone with a tape recorder could have produced a marvelous document on the poetic process.

And old magics could be reborn. Once, at the New York City Ballet (an evening when Villella had been especially breathtaking), I ran into Paul Engle during intermission. Much of my rancor had abated; he seemed changed. His wife had been committed, then died; he had married a Chinese woman whom many admired and who adored him. He had lost the Workshops at Iowa; taking his funds with him, he had initiated an International Translations Center, something unique in the academic world. Yet that serious defeat, and surely the change in his affectional life, had made him humbler, more humane. We planned to meet later for a drink.

Coming out of Lincoln Center together, we ran into Lowell on the street. Their enmity, too, seemed to have faded. On my book jacket Lowell had described Iowa—in a sharp slash at Engle—as the "most sterile of sterile places." I later discovered that, several years before, Engle had been suddenly hospitalized while in New York. Lowell had visited him there and they had grown friendly again. Each now seemed thoughtful of the other's feelings: Engle carefully stepping around difficult subjects; Lowell, in his heavy-handed way, blundering into painful areas but turning quickly to put an apologetic hand on Engle's sleeve or make a counterbalancing compliment. Lowell suggested we go to his place at the Dakota for a drink; when I said that my wife, Camille, was coming in on a plane around midnight, he suggested that I pick her up and join them there.

When we arrived, both were busily conjuring up the greats of the past generation—Engle recalling that after Robert Frost's son had killed himself, Engle walked the beaches of Cuba with Frost, talking him out of suicide. "How little good," Frost had said, "my health has ever done for anyone dear to me."

Lowell told of being with Pound when he first heard of Eliot's death. Pound responded with three statements, each delivered, after a pause, in a different voice: first, the official pronouncement, "My old comrade in the arts is dead." Then, the voice of personal loss and half-humorous complaint, "Now, who will understand my jokes?" And finally, a rush to generous acknowledgment and praise, but in the voice an Idahoan would use speaking of a horse trainer or auto mechanic: "Well, you've got to admit he was one *hell* of a poet!"

It was one of the evenings of a lifetime. It was punctuated, however, at roughly forty-five minute intervals by the appearance of Lowell's wife, Elizabeth Hardwick, on the balcony above their two-story living room. Once again in nightgown and socks, she would peer over the railing like a figure on a medieval clock tower, calling, "Cal! Cal! Don't you know the time? You'll be an absolute wreck!" Camille, Engle, and I would get up, embarrassed, and tiptoe for the door. But as soon as she was out of sight, Lowell would wink and whisper us back for just one more drink. Even knowing how difficult Lowell could be to himself and, surely, to his wife, who could resist such talk and such company? There we would be for the next incarnation forty-five minutes later.

That was not the last time I saw Lowell, but things were never so rich again. Gradually, I thought, his work was losing force and direction. Above all, he seemed unable to find the feel of his own passions, became as gray and indecisive as that father he describes in his poems. With the passions went the voice—he showed me poems which tried to recapture the wildness of the earliest poems, the clarities of *Life Studies*, or any defined voice. In time, he became the center of an industry, surrounded by sycophants or those founding careers on his. Acclaim grew as the poems diminished and he declined, I thought, into a public figure.

After our last meeting, there were a few letters—chiefly about his divorce and remarriage to Caroline Blackwood in England, a life that he detailed rapturously. It seemed improbable that this could last. Back in New York again, he died shortly before his taxi reached Hardwick's apartment. During their separation, he had used her private letters in his poems—an act which I, like many others, thought execrable. It is no doubt a failing that I have never ended a marriage amicably—love converts too easily into hatred—but I, too, would have died before going back into the apartment of someone I had once loved but then had so profoundly injured.

As for Jarrell, he remained as outrageous in manner, as brilliant in perception. When I was teaching in Detroit, he came for a visit; he read, among other things, his translation of Goethe's *Faust*. He was the best Gretchen I ever heard; there wasn't a dry eye in the house. Later that day, I took the Jarrells to the Detroit Institute of Art where he soon found a wild and mangy cat by Kokoschka; guards stared, aghast, as he called to his wife at the end of the gallery, "Pussycat! Come see the kitty!"

Although in general we became friendlier, I tended to keep my distance, knowing how cutting he could be to anything less than total acquiescence. Several times, he had sliced me to ribbons: once, at a party I had given for him at my Iowa barracks apartment; once at the opening of a Lowell play in New York. I had come in to review *The Old Glory* for *The New York Review of Books*. At the party onstage after the opening, Jarrell collared me: "That's one of the half-dozen best plays ever written in America. Isn't it?" I answered that I liked it very much; not *that* much. For weeks, I licked my wounds.

Jealousy, I think, was a crucial problem for Jarrell; he could scarcely have felt anything less for the force of the play, for Lowell's public position, his standing in New York's intellectual and artistic circles. Jarrell lived in Greensboro, North Carolina, and his power-fully moving poems were ignored. But jealousy was a quality he could not forgive himself and it played a factor, I suspect, in his final breakdown. It must have been difficult to accept the two daughters of his second wife, Mary—once he *had* accepted them, even harder to accept their maturity and loss. Even more significant, of course, must have been the death of his mother.

In any case, he, the one poet of that generation I'd thought might escape madness, was hospitalized too. His cleverness was surely a hindrance: I am told he could usually talk his way around his doctors. I think this same quality contributed to a falling away in the later poems—it took something as fearsome as the war to shock him into seriousness, away from displays of wit and elegance that could provide a way out. Back home, on leave from the hospital, he was struck by a sports car. He had driven a Maserati himself; whether or not he chose the one that killed him, he would have wanted a worthy destroyer. His wife, who had not been present, long insisted his death was an accident; I've met no one else who thought so. Lowell, Jarrell, Schwartz, Roethke, Berryman—a whole generation of gifted but dangerously driven poets—had each in turn passed into fearful neuroses, usually involving bad behavior, drunkenness, new girl friends, deaths which suggested no great urge toward a longer life. Jarrell's loss was particularly tragic; a rich career might still have lain ahead. We were deprived not only of a superbly creative and moving poet, but an original, daring mind and probably our best critic.

As for John Berryman, I didn't merely avoid, I practically fled him—he was too dangerous. After pawing the wife of a well-known younger poet and former student all one evening, he had struck the man over the head with a full whiskey bottle (which could easily have killed him), then jumped on him, breaking a rib. Once, visiting

Detroit, he managed to get my lady friend in the backseat of a car, my wife and myself in the front. Instantly alert to the hazards, he began pursuing the lady around the back seat. Hearing her protests, I stopped the car and said, "John, this is a proper lady who does not like to be mauled." "What?" he said, "You mean you don't fuck?" Everyone gasped. "Oh! It's that word. That's what bothers you, the word: P-H-U-Q-Q. I promise never to use that word again." We all dissolved into giggling. Such little-boy-naughtiness may be amusing to recount afterward; it might have seriously damaged a number of people, some of them innocent.

I did hazard his company once more: this time, *I* almost injured *him*. Arriving in Los Angeles for a reading, I was met at the plane by my old friend, Henri Coulette. He grabbed me by the arm, glared in my eye and snarled, "Listen, you son of a bitch, you try anything and I'll kill you." "Hank, what did I do?" I gasped. "Nothing," he said. "We've had Berryman here for a week and I just can't stand any more trouble." All week, Berryman had refused to sleep or eat, stayed up all night monologuing, collapsed during readings, went to hospitals, propositioned the nurses, roamed the corridors, went back out against doctors' orders, collapsed again. Everyone was frantic. Now he was at the Green Hotel in Pasadena, watched over by students.

At the door of his room I was greeted by a young woman built roughly like a hydrant, with a great shock of black hair and arms thick as my waist. "Hi," she said in a gravelly baritone, holding out her hand. "My name is Vivian Cienfuegos. I'm lookin' afta John. If he gets outa bed, I belt 'im in the chops!" She knew how funny that was. Tough and savvy, she was a sociology student, and immune to the reverence which had made the job impossible for several shifts of literature students, recruited as temporary nursing staff to protect Berryman from Berryman. Every time he reared off the bed with some obscene proposal, she laid a massive forearm upon him, delivering him safely to the mat. When he awoke and spoke to me, not realizing how frail he was, I thumped him on the chest. He fell back, choking and coughing uncontrollably. She and I looked at each other, terrified. He did recover enough to be sent back to his wife; Vivian, in large part, was responsible. He mentions her, gratefully, in a poem but neither he nor the literary world gave her half the thanks she deserved.

I kept away after that. His case was the most frightening of all. I knew that many brilliant men's achievements and problems centered around their attachments to difficult and powerful mothers. Only after I'd read John Haffenden's and Eileen Simpson's books on Berryman did I realize this was even truer for him than for the others. I *did* know I didn't want to see this brilliant poet throwing away his life and energies either in childish nastiness or in being rescued and nursed back to life by avatars, comic or tragic, of his mother. The only literary lessons left lay in the print of his poems; the extra-literary lessons were too fierce to learn close by. It is only surprising he lasted so long before stepping off that bridge in Minneapolis.

I finally met William Empson in the '70s, when I had long imagined him to be dead. He had been living in England but an economic crisis had forced him out of retirement. At the University of Delaware, where I taught and where he came as a Visiting Distinguished Professor, I met him at a party given by Kay and Gibbons Ruark. He no longer wore the great spade-shaped beard I had seen in photos; he no longer smoked a pipe and cigarette at the same time. When I told him how much his poems had meant to me, he seemed not quite sure what I meant.

Later that evening, I met his wife: a large woman, somewhat younger. When I told her how long I had admired and wanted to meet Empson, she replied, "Well, you *may* have been in time." All evening she spoke with maximum disrespect for him and maximum aggression against everyone else, especially if they displayed any interest in him. The insult aside, her remark was true enough; I may have exaggerated in saying I met William Empson. He came to life only for a moment at the mention of Marlowe's *Faustus* and talked shrewdly about its probable political censorship. Then he fell back into fog, maundered aimlessly or stood silent on the borders of conversation.

Just as I was going home, he happened also to leave the house, following his wife and another man. There were rumors that in England her lover lived with them and that Empson usually got up to make their breakfast. It was drizzling; as he hurried across the lawn to catch up, she shouted, "Bill! Bill! Get out of that grass. You'll catch a dreadful cold! Have you no sense at all?"

IX. DABBLING IN CORRUPTION

E. E. Cummings once wrote a nasty little jingle:

> mr. u will not be missed
> who as an anthologist
> sold the many on the few
> not excluding mr. u

I don't know what had roused Cummings' ire; he was fairly well represented in Untermeyer's anthologies. Untermeyer sometimes overlooked a great poem, seldom a good one. He *did* print some of his own poems, which were not terrible—also his several wives' poems, which *were*. Still, if unforgivable, that seemed unavoidable. Personally, I was indebted to him and had found him lively, witty, and engaging.

What's more, he *was* missed; Oscar Williams took his place. Reviewing Williams' *Little Treasury of Modern Poetry*, Randall Jarrell remarked that "the book has the merit of having a considerably larger selection of Oscar Williams' poems than . . . any other anthology. . . . It takes great courage to like your own poetry almost twice as much as Hardy's." At the anthology's next printing (not even the next edition), a copy turned up in Jarrell's mailbox. In it, he found a marker at the place where his own poems *had* been.

Largely because of this exclusion from Williams' collections (soon standard for college courses) Jarrell is still less well-known than such contemporaries as Lowell or Roethke, though for me he is a stronger poet. It is sharply ironic that Williams continued to use exactly those poems by Hardy and Whitman—both dismissed by Eliot and in disrepute—which Jarrell had singled out in earlier essays. Thus, Jarrell was able to restore the reputation of two marvelous poets through his influence on Williams; himself he could not save.

Untermeyer had published his several wives' poems. Williams had only one wife, Gene Derwood—dead some years before I met him—but went more than double to promote her. Her poems were in his anthology; her picture (doctored, I'm told, to improve the complexion) inside the cover, cheek by jowl with Pound, Yeats, and Eliot.

My friend, the writer George P. Elliott, once encountered Williams at a cocktail party in New York. Obsessively punctual, George was the first to arrive; Williams, the second. They had to talk to each other: "Well, Mr. Elliott, I enjoyed your anthology," said Williams, referring to a collection George had recently edited. "I see only two things wrong with it: you don't have any poems by me or by my wife." No rejoinder suggested itself; Williams continued: "You do know the poems of Gene Derwood?" George lied that he did not. "Well, you won't mind if I send you a copy of her book?" George lied again, wondering what to do with *this* copy.

Just then, someone really important entered the room and Williams started toward him. But then he turned back, his hand extended: "And I do hope I'll be able to include some of *your* poems in *my* next anthology?"

Shortly after my first book, *Heart's Needle*, appeared, I realized that we had neglected to send Williams a copy, though he had expressed an interest. I wrote my publisher, Knopf, asking who should take care of that. They, who liked to appear above such considerations, replied that they didn't know but it certainly wasn't *them*! I knew Williams' reputation, yet he'd done me no harm and his support might be important. I asked Knopf to send him a book, charge it to me, and put in a card "Compliments of the Author"— I couldn't get myself to sign it.

It was like dropping, at one step, from a concrete sidewalk into waist-deep muck. Every week something new arrived in *my* mailbox—Williams' book, his wife's book, a recording for which Williams had coerced various literary figures to read her poems, postcards displaying her hideous portrait busts of Dylan Thomas, of Robert Frost, of Oscar himself, each marked "On Loan to Harvard University until the Year 2000," photo-postcards showing Williams with important personages. One day, a specially odious card arrived showing him with Dylan Thomas, both squinting against a strong light as if they had just crept out of a pub or from under a log.

My stepdaughter carried this into the house as if with tweezers, saying, "Ooooooo! When did *they* die?"

I think I did not begin to suspect the varieties of decadence that surround "po-biz" until I was invited to The National Poetry Festival held at the Library of Congress in Washington, D.C., during the early 1960s. The poetry commissars were there—editors, anthologists, directors of writing programs—all scheduled to read their poems to each other. There were also poets. J. V. Cunningham said, over a glass of bourbon, "It's just like a cozy MLA meeting; dogs sniffing each other's haunches. Only, here, no one knows what job he's brown-nosing for!" Randall and Mary Jarrell surveyed one of the official meetings with disgust, then alarm, when they noticed a female reporter from the BBC carrying a Nagra tape recorder. "We'll grab her," he said, "you run with the recorder. No evidence of this must ever get out of the country!"

I would not try to persuade you that poets, gathered at such conferences, or out on the poetry-reading circuits, are less lecherous (or less anxious to *seem* lecherous) than other traveling salesmen. Farmers' daughters and poetry groupies lurk in many a landscape. An artist must keep open his or her senses and emotions—a doctrine liable to self-serving interpretations and in no case conducive to placid relations with spouses and lovers. And such unquiet relations make one only the more susceptible to temptations. Many male poets feel they must live down the image of artist as wimp, or else live down *to* the myth of artist as *hero maudit*, perishing of debauch, drink or dementia. That suicidal myth was helping decimate the poets of the generation before mine—say, Dylan Thomas through John Berryman—who, in turn, passed it on to the female poets of the next.

Everyone knows pretty much who will be invited to conferences; everyone waits to see who those invited will invite. Some arrive with wives or husbands, even their own, as did Richard Wilbur. Some appear with more or less permanent lovers; Delmore Schwartz brought a very young woman with whom he then lived in Syracuse (as his dementia deepened, he kept a number of young women in apartments scattered throughout that city). Williams, though alone on this occasion, usually came to conferences with one of the most voluptuous-looking women I ever met. Tall and rangy, she had long blond hairs growing on the rims of her ears; her name suggested descent from the minor Hungarian nobility. Some years later, I ran into her on the streets of San Francisco and enjoyed the unearned appearance of splendorous debauchery by riding around town with her in a fire-engine red MG or turning up for breakfast at Fanny's Floating Restaurant in Sausalito. Williams took her to several MLA meetings, where he introduced her as a medievalist; it was said she, although a ceramist, had received offers from two major universities.

Others arrived with hopes. You'd meet both the polished seducer totting up his scorecard and the rougher "good ol' boy" who pinched hard, apparently fearful that his brutally lewd propositionings might be accepted. Often, too, the mischief-maker who, if he liked you, would try openly to seduce your wife. And equally restless female poets. Early on at this conference, I was approached by a somewhat older, gifted and attractive woman poet whom I had always liked. I wish I could say that a sense of honor, not the glamour of a younger woman, dissuaded me.

When I had first arrived in the D.C. train station, I ran into a young woman, a student I'd known at Wayne State in Detroit. She'd been sleeping on the station benches and subsisting on coffee and apples while waiting for a train that was still two days away. Once I was signed-in and settled, I went back to invite her to the conference—there would be lots of food and drink, she could hear and meet the big-name poets and stay with me in the hotel. This, of course, infuriated everyone—and I did nothing to dispel their assumptions. I'd have been delighted if something sexual *had* developed; it didn't. She enjoyed the conference; I enjoyed her company—and the envy it provoked. I overheard someone saying, in tones of outrage, "He's got a girl even younger than Delmore's!"

Such envy is easy to rouse and can serve as a substitute for recognition of one's work. Once, at the request of a colleague, I escorted a handsome young woman, whom I'd barely met, to a conference at Colgate University. This so enraged my fellow conferees James Dickey and Norman Mailer that they nearly had a fistfight with each other—each apparently seeing me as an unworthy opponent. In San Francisco I once took a woman—also very handsome though nearer my own age—to a party. Days later, an argument there erupted over whether she (actually the daughter of a Greek gambler) had been a countess or a princess. Casual sex can easily be overrated; its repute and the jealousies it brings offer surer, though no safer, delights.

As for Delmore and his young girlfriend, they got into a quarrel in their Washington hotel room—he was already far into paranoia and madness. When she fled down the hall to spend the night with Richard Wilbur and his wife, Delmore began breaking up the furniture and was carted away by the police. The next day I asked Richard what had happened; he said only, "Delmore. He hurt his room." Meantime, John Berryman, drunk and outrageous as usual, had gone down to the station to get Delmore out, but (perhaps jealous of his notoriety) had instead got himself thrown in, too. We had to persuade Richard Eberhart, a former Navy lieutenant commander now clad in a business suit, tie, and ponderous respectability, to go down and liberate both. A delicious aftereffect was to receive, several weeks later, a letter from Berryman (who assumed my ignorance of the backstage maneuvers) telling me how *he* had rescued Delmore.

Whether he rescued Delmore or not, Berryman did save the conference, providing its only really creditable moment: the first general public reading of the *Dream Songs*. The audience was electrified; Allen Tate, who did not habitually applaud others' work, bellowed, "Bravo, John!" Otherwise, the meetings crawled on in disgrace; most of us busied ourselves otherwhere.

I had gone off on a strange project. Back in Detroit, a friend and I had been writing a play about the local John Robert Powers School of Modeling where she had been a teacher. We had interviewed a number of people formerly connected with the school—including a lady who unwittingly told me how she had murdered her husband. I'd had to block all response so completely that the information itself vanished from my mind for several days.

Now, in Washington, I decided to try the local Powers School to see what facts might be co-opted for our play. Two poets from the conference, Anthony Ostroff and Oswald LeWinter (a master of disguise and gentle con games), jumped at the opportunity. We took, for ourselves, names of editors at *The Saturday Evening Post*, found the address in the phone book and set off for the beauty school. This, sadly, came to nothing—the school itself, apparently, was so deep in corruption (or at least in debt) that it had closed its doors and its owners had quietly disappeared. A neighbor told us that someone came in the dead of night to collect mail.

Our attempt to con the con artists had fizzled out. Yet there on the street outside the locked beauty school we ran into Oscar Williams, out on a project of his own—a phonograph record of poets reading their own work. I should probably have felt honored that he wanted to include me; what I *did* feel was suspicion. I had made one recording for the Library of Congress that was poorly engineered and on which I had read abominably. I wanted time to improve my reading, to check the quality of this recording, check opportunities to rerecord, find out who else might be involved. And whether someone less predatory than Williams mightn't be making a competing record. I thought I had a perfect out; I told Williams I couldn't commit myself until I finished a recording I'd promised my British publisher. This was true enough, even if *not* the real reason. Apparently satisfied, he invited us all to a party at his hotel that evening after the final poetry reading by Robert Frost. Perhaps we could talk about it then, he said; I hoped, foolishly, he might forget about it.

In the meantime, fiercer events were unfolding which suggested that even if we arrived at Frost's reading or Williams' party, none of us might live to tell our friends or families. Our luncheon with Jacqueline Kennedy that day was suddenly cancelled—rumor had it she was in a cave somewhere in a western state. Soviet ships carrying nuclear missiles were steaming toward Cuba; if they tried to run our blockade of that island, World War III would almost certainly begin; Washington would be wiped out in hours.

Not surprisingly, this cast a greenish and terminal glow over the remaining meetings and cocktail parties. At one of those I met, for the first and the last time, Robert Frost, eighty-eight and obviously in his last months. We spoke for a few moments but said nothing. He did not mention, and perhaps did not recall, that a few weeks before he had attacked me during his reading in Detroit. Some of my students had earlier asked him about my interpretations of his poems; from the platform, he had issued scathing remarks about academics who thought "Stopping by Woods" had something to do with death or suicide. Two days later, though, he read the same poem in Ann Arbor, about forty-five miles away, then looked up, startled, to say, "Well, now, that *does* have a good deal of the ultimate about it, doesn't it?" An Oedipal moment—he had so long falsified his poem that he'd forgotten when and why he wrote it. Yet, like Oedipus, he was capable of piercing even his own smoke screen. After that encounter, then his more recent appearance at Kennedy's inauguration, I was naturally curious about what might happen at his reading at the Library that evening, an event with even more of the ultimate about it.

After the cocktail party where I had met Frost, we all had to find dinner. Earlier, I'd been approached by a reporter from *Time* who wanted to interview me and suggested that the young woman and I should join him and his expense account. As we piled into a cab, the driver said, "I guess I'll get my uniform out of mothballs." I thought, "You won't have time to change your socks!" But then I decided—already quite drunk from trying to shut out the air of general sleaziness and impending doom—that at least I'd die in *my own* uniform. Stopping the cab, I got out and tore a long vine off the high stone wall of some institute's garden, wove and awarded myself, like Lvborg, a crown of vine leaves.

The cab took us—where else?—to Trader Vic's. Entering, I handed my crown of vines to the hatcheck girl. She never blinked; attaching a small cardboard number, she set it on the shelf beside the homburgs and military dress caps. In a flower-festooned concrete nook, sitting with a young woman I scarcely knew but with whom I was ostensibly sleeping, I ate coconut-coated shrimp and drank, through two-foot straws, syrupy hooch from a vast, gardenia-decorated bowl—paid for by a magazine I did not respect but whose praise I wanted, via the plastic card held by a man whose name I did not know. Meanwhile, from upstairs, we could hear the televised voice of John Kennedy saying that we would soon know whether Western Civilization might continue. As we left, I fished the gardenias from the empty bowl to pin on the young woman's dress, but forgot to reclaim my crown of vines. Sometimes, when I am back in Washington, I imagine it still sitting forlorn among the fedoras and uniform caps of another generation.

If that had seemed lurid, Robert Frost's reading entirely outdid it. By this time, I was even more drunk and—as with my earlier Powers School interview in Detroit—did not dare register what was happening until a day or so later. Frost began, as he almost never did, by reading someone else's poem: "Shine, Perishing Republic" by Robinson Jeffers. The title alone might have outraged his audience, but they were so preconditioned to reverence that nothing else could reach them. Moving to his own poem, "October," he drew special attention to its relevance for the current autumnal crisis:

> O hushed October morning mild,
> The leaves have ripened to the fall;
> Tomorrow's wind, if it be wild,
> Should waste them all.

His next poem, "November," developed that figure:

> We saw leaves go to glory,
>
> And then to end the story
> Get beaten down and pasted
> In one wild day of rain.
> We heard "'Tis over" roaring.
> A year of leaves was wasted.
> Oh, we make a boast of storing
> Of saving and of keeping,
> But only by ignoring
> ....
> By denying and ignoring
> The waste of nations warring.

He said that this was no waste "if it's toward some meaning. But you can call it waste, you can call it expense. Just for this evening." Then he added a new line of his own:

> By denying and ignoring
> The waste of nations warring
> And the waste of breath deploring.

This was a direct slap at those whose attitude toward the crisis differed from his. In him, it produced an immediate exhilaration and pugnacity—not against the Russians or Krushchev (whom he called "the greatest ruler in the world, you know, the almighty") but against the liberals—most of his audience. They had often criticized his politics (e.g., his saying that we shouldn't get rid of the poor since he needed them in his work), and throughout the evening he kept gibing at their attitudes in general and, specifically, toward this crisis. He spoke of "Dover Beachcombers" and those who "would rather fuss with a Gordian knot than cut it." He went on to say that "every liberal that I know of has a tendency when his enemy works up against him, . . . to try to remember if he isn't more in the wrong than the enemy . . . a liberal is a person who can't take his own side in a fight." As the evening went on, he began pumping himself up and down behind the lectern like a rooster about to crow. Breaking into what seemed a laugh, he referred to that fearful crisis exultantly, "You didn't want to just fade out, did you? Why not go out in a blaze of glory?"

After he had received a standing ovation and everyone started to leave, he returned to the podium and called us all back to make some inconsequential comment. He received a second standing ovation and everyone started to leave. And once again, he called everyone back for another empty comment and a third standing ovation.

All this time, R. P. Blackmur, sitting near me, was growling loud obscenities: "You dirty old bastard! You rotten . . ." Though I'd heard Blackmur had never liked Frost, this seemed strange. As we surged out of the hall, myself leading the young girl by the hand, I was astonished to hear myself loudly singing an old Scottish ballad:

She was trantin' and dancin' and singin' for joy;
She's vowed that very night she would feast Inverey;
She hae laugh' wi' him, danced wi' him, carried him ben;
She was kind wi' the villain that had slain her guid man.

I had no notion why either Blackmur or I were behaving so badly. Days later I asked myself why I had been singing *that* song— "The Baron o' Brackley." Earlier in the song, Brackley, head of the clan Gordon, had been prodded by his wife to ride out to fight a pack of hired cattle thieves and gallows birds who finally slaughter him. Now, triumphing in his death, she spends the night with Inverey, the gang's leader. Only when I had run through the whole song did I realize how betrayed I had felt by Frost's speech and his attitude. Of all the people in that packed hall, only Blackmur had recognized that Frost was not only triumphing over those in his audience he thought overscrupulous, but laughing at the probability of that audience's imminent death. Now he would not have to die alone; he had had his full career: they would not. Meantime, they were so worshipful that he could mock them to their faces and receive, in return, not one but three standing ovations.

From Frost's reading, as if that weren't eerie enough, we went to Oscar Williams' suite. There we found Richard Wilbur and sat, literally, at his feet, feeling he was an island of reason in this wide sea of sham and corruption. Before long, though, Williams himself appeared and began badgering me again about his recording. I reminded him of my earlier answer—that I must first fulfill my commitment to my British publisher. "Well," he said, getting up, "Mr. Snodgrass is talking through his hat again." This held just enough truth to infuriate me. I followed behind him, saying loudly, "We want our coats; we are going home." To my surprise, he turned suddenly affable, put his arm around me and said, "Oh, come now, surely you can take a joke. Come on back and have a drink." Wandering back to Richard Wilbur, happily bemused, I thought I had won. Williams, it seemed, must think me either a very good poet or else very influential to back off from me in his own hotel suite. Seldom have I been able to summon that kind of immediate aggressive response; apparent success had made me quite smug.

A week or so later—back home with my wife and children, the Poetry Festival and the Cuban Crisis safely, I thought, behind me—I found in my mailbox a letter with no return address but postmarked New York City. Inside was a snapshot of the young girl and myself sitting at the feet of Richard Wilbur. The only comment, scribbled on the back, seemed conciliatory, yet there was also a clear, if unspoken, message: "Get frisky and I can cause you a lot of trouble." I had wondered, earlier, how Williams convinced so many well-known people to record his wife's turgid poetry; that no longer seemed so mysterious. It did begin to seem that I—a dabbler in corruption, one who liked the look of profligacy—had no business challenging professionals.

Others learned at greater cost. The Hungarian ceramist, tough and savvy, could take care of herself; she was easily a match for Williams. Rumors said, however, that others close to her, shyer, less wary, more vulnerable, got pregnant and were dumped. Whether the rumors were true or not, and though I scarcely feared *that* sort of misconception, I realized that others near me, too, could be damaged. If Dickey and Mailer recognized me, instantly, as hors de combat, I had to recognize that I was no match for Williams, either. In any market, the small investor is, by definition, the losing investor.

It seemed a telling coincidence that this conference had been held in Washington, D.C. If people *do* deserve the governments they get—can anyone really be *that* undeserving?—they must also deserve their literary culture. A people unable to produce a society where loyalty might tend downward as well as up, unable to produce a statesman or ruler concerned with their welfare, could hardly expect to produce a literary politician more gifted or devoted. Yet it seemed needlessly shameful that such a man as Williams should define the quality of our literary life—which poets would be read, which acclaimed, which would get awards and grants, which would have a "career." We were sure that

mr. double-u would not be missed

127

and hoped for the day he would die or be superseded as a power. Naive, learning nothing from the deposal of mr. u, we assumed that after mr. double-u, things would *have* to get better.

X. BALKAN SONGS

In 1960, soon after I received the Pulitzer Prize, I got a call from the State Department's United States Information Service, offering to send me to the Edinburgh Festival to give a poetry reading. I told my caller he should know that I was unsympathetic to American foreign policy. He said that was all right—naturally, they'd prefer that I not attack their policies while they were paying my bills, but would suggest only that I needn't seek political discussions; I was being sent for artistic, not political, reasons. I tended to doubt that, but had no great desire to argue policies in any case. Other writers who'd gone on such occasions seemed to see them as an honor. This would be my first time outside the United States since Saipan; I decided to go.

From the first, Edinburgh felt right—my family had come from that area; soon my ears were filled again with Scottish voices and Scottish music. In the Festival Fringe that year was a one-man show about Bobby Burns, my ancestor without benefit of clergy. I had already caught Burns's interest in folk songs and ballads and found, at the Festival, the nearly blind folksinger Frankie Armstrong, who lived with her accompanist, a classical guitarist. I'm not sure whether I more coveted her dark, clear voice or her person. We became fast friends; ever since, we've written letters and, whenever we could get into the same country at the same time, went to each other's performances and sat up nights to talk. Lucky, perhaps, that we never became lovers!

In Edinburgh, I did the obligatory things—toured the castle, prowled the ominous, twisting streets, was awed by the smoke-stained, overbearing architecture. I shopped for my girlfriend—my second marriage was already dissolving—and for my children, who were again being kept from me. I discovered scones, shortbread, finnan haddie for breakfast, kidney pie for lunch and, above all, single malt liquors by day or night—they hadn't yet been introduced to most of the U.S.

Of course, I attended Festival events. That year there were two Macbeths: the first, a production in the round of the "Scottish Play."

Theorizing, perhaps, that evil should be attractive, the director had decided to have his witches played by three notably sleek and graceful young women clad only in small, gray pubic wigs. Having struck upon this admirable idea, he also had them appear in nearly all important scenes, handing the actors goblets, swords, luring or pushing them this way or that, generally controlling the action. Newspaper critics dubbed this "Macbeth *au go-go*." Meantime, the second Macbeth—George MacBeth, the British poet who had helped organize this, the Festival's first poetry reading—strolled about the Festival headquarters, cheerfully proposing to sleep with every young woman who appeared. "Auld Reeky" appeared not to be all smoke and Protestant gloom, after all.

From the first, I got on with the Scottish poets. One noon, I wandered into the pub where I'd heard they hung out. There they were, around one large table, talking and laughing convivially. An outsider, I took a small table alone and ordered my steak and kidney pie. To my astonishment, the sovereign of that larger round table, Hugh MacDiarmid—whose presence chiefly had daunted me—rose, came over to my table, introduced himself, and invited me to join them. Within three minutes, we were all old friends.

A conspiracy was afoot to exclude one of their own best-known poets, Sydney Goodsir Smith, who sat alone at a small table like the one I'd just left. What was wrong with Smith, I asked. Oh, nothing's wrong with him, I was told; we all love him, but he'll get MacDiarmid drunk—that could kill the old man. Of course, Smith *did* join us—he and MacDiarmid were very close. MacDiarmid complained that he couldn't visit the United States because his wife feared he'd get tangled up with American girls as Dylan Thomas had. I never heard a gentler or sweeter boast—both of his own potency, and of his wife's care. At closing time (bars were shut from 2 till 4 lest the economy collapse), we sent him home to his wife, safe from American girls and from Smith's alcoholic blandishments.

We were, ourselves, less well secured. Smith proposed that we take the half-hour taxi ride out to the Firth of Forth Bridge. All the way there and back, he kept reaching into hidden crannies in his clothing—the breast pocket, down the back of the collar—and extracting pint bottles of Scotch which, a supposed precaution against the blustery weather, were passed around the crowded cab. As each in turn was emptied, he'd fish into some other corner of his garb and produce a successor.

It was the Brits that I (like the Scots) didn't get along with. There were to be readings on two successive evenings, each involving six or eight poets, the whole arranged and emceed by the novelist and journalist John Wain. I read on the first evening; this got good reviews, so I was asked to read again the next evening. I had, however, already read my best work and didn't want to repeat that program. I asked if I could read a truly great American poem—"Out of the Cradle Endlessly Rocking." I had recently discovered just how marvelous it was and wanted others to know. My hosts asked how long that would take—about twenty minutes, I told them. The problem was that Auden would read last that evening and had been given a longer segment than the others; my twenty minutes might eat into that. They promised, however, to ask the BBC, who were broadcasting the reading, for an extension. When that was granted, I went ahead with the Whitman.

Afterward, I found the backstage in an uproar—Stevie Smith had been making venomous accusations that I had usurped their time. Auden had withdrawn to his dressing room, threatening not to read at all. "What's he yelling about out there?" he'd demanded. Wain and others had explained the situation to both Auden and Smith, but that had not placated them. I went myself to Auden, explained why I'd wanted to read this poem but that I deeply respected his work and had taken care not to encroach on his time. He would have exactly what he'd been promised—merely a few minutes later than originally scheduled. For my trouble, I got a scowl and a grunt.

* * *

As I was settling down back in Detroit, the State Department called again to ask if I'd like to go to Russia on a similar tour. Two weeks later they called again to say the trip had been called off. As part of the Cold War finagling, the Russians had to pretend to be outraged by our involvement in Vietnam (actually, nothing could have pleased them more), so they had canceled the rest of the cultural exchange policy for that year. Clearly, they weren't very angry—all that remained of it were *Hello, Dolly!* and me!

I tried not to be too upset about missing Russia—friends who had been there had hated it. Besides, my wife was furious that I would be going alone. Strong tensions had arisen between us since (and largely because of) the Pulitzer Prize. While poor and frantically driven we had gotten along splendidly, had been helpful and generous to each other. But when outside pressures eased, we started making new ones, turned grasping and faithless. If I didn't go to Russia, things might at least have a chance to quiet down.

In another two weeks, the State Department called again: would I like, instead, to visit some smaller Iron Curtain countries—Hungary, Romania, perhaps Czechoslovakia and Yugoslavia, perhaps Bulgaria—then come back by way of Vienna, Berlin, Paris, and Lisbon? As for the Balkan countries, I was almost totally ignorant. But what better way to learn?

At the USIS in Washington, I found that I would visit Bulgaria, Romania, and Hungary. They weren't sure whether I could get into Yugoslavia or Czechoslovakia since they'd recently sent Allen Ginsberg and the Czechs might not tolerate another American poet. It seemed I *could* get into Bulgaria, though (or perhaps because) no American had been sent there for ten years. I was told that I wouldn't much like Sofia in Bulgaria or Bucharest in Romania— they were poor and Stalinist. I would like Budapest in Hungary a little better since it was more like a Western capital. Then I'd go on to Vienna, Berlin, Paris, Lisbon and have a marvelous time. It worked out quite the other way around.

There was no problem with my entry into Bulgaria; the American cultural attaché met me at Sofia's airport, helped me through customs, and took me to a huge, old-fashioned luxury hotel where I slept in a bed like a large, polished, hardwood coffin. Otherwise, everything had an odd familiarity. Sofia seemed much like the small industrial city near Pittsburgh where I'd grown up. The air was full of coal smoke from the factories and furnaces; freight trains wailed from the outskirts. There were dark, squarish autos and clanking trolleys in the streets that were otherwise half-deserted. One young woman from the American mission (we did not have a full-fledged embassy) told me of her mother's worries that she was in a far-off, dangerous, Communist country; she had answered that, if she came home to Washington, she wouldn't dare list her phone in the public book and, if she ever had a sleepless night, wouldn't dare take a walk. Here she could walk anywhere in the city, day or night.

At one of the first functions, I met Vlada Dimitrova, "the Bulgarian Poetess" about whom John Updike had written, and on whom he had apparently developed a crush. Easy to see why—she seemed the only attractive or well-dressed woman in the country. Most worked at menial jobs—hotel maids and waitresses, street cleaners, masons, etc.—and dressed the part. Vlada Dimitrova, though a dedicated Communist, wore makeup, the latest Western fashions, and had her blond hair (uncommon there) in a high, artificial do.

I asked my host, the cultural attaché, if I might invite her to the theater (she had very good English) and he consented; so did she. When I asked where I might call for her (in a taxi, I had supposed), she replied that she would, of course, call for me in an official car with a state driver. (To record the gist of our conversation, I later realized.) That quashed any faint imaginings I may have had of a romantic encounter.

Moreover, I made a serious public gaffe at the theater. The play was Max Frisch's *Biedermann and the Firebugs,* which I had just translated into English, collaborating first with Lore Segal, then with Rosmarie Waldrop. Though I could never secure permission for either publication or performance, I admired the play and wanted to see how it would fare in a Bulgarian translation and performance. It was a fine production, well-set and -costumed, free of the tricks and extraneous stagy business American producers usually inserted to cover the dreary authorized translation by Mordecai Gorelik. I could catch most of the sense from knowing the original and from the actors' very lively delivery. It was at the hilarious presentation of one such line that I committed my indiscretion: I laughed. The whole audience turned to stare. Miss Dimitrova informed me, politely, that Bulgarians do not laugh in the theater, however funny the play!

I probably should have guessed that; they were the most serious people I had ever met. They did not equate happiness with idleness or "fun" as we did; they didn't even equate it with their own hard work. You couldn't say they *were* happy; they simply seemed content. Perhaps they felt this was part of their Slav heritage. They felt akin to the Russians, who had twice saved them from invaders; besides, they had Romania acting as a buffer between their two countries.

Actually, you saw surprisingly few Bulgarians: they were either at work or in their houses—you only saw them passing from one to the other. My hosts—Americans who surely had little reason to exaggerate the contentment of any communist society—said that Bulgarians seemed not to desire fine clothes, fine houses or furniture, luxuries: they invested their lives in their landscape. Every stone of every street and highway had been laid by hand in a fishscale pattern which, as you drove, seemed to fan out before you. On both sides of every major roadway, equidistant from each other, stood small ornamental trees, each painted white to exactly the same height. Somewhat farther apart stood uniformed militiamen, each holding his rifle at "port arms"—apparently ever since he came on duty. They looked so immobile, one wondered if a careless (or rebellious) highway crewman didn't occasionally paint one of them white to the same height as the trees. Every rock of the landscape might have been taken up, dusted, numbered, listed in an official archive, then replaced.

Their attitude has had its rewards. In the communal fields, farmers drove tractors under a strange system of plastic "roofs"— a method that captured the whole Mediterranean market for tomatoes. When I returned briefly, some twenty-five years later, their smoke-belching factories had brought prosperity to the whole country, though their pollution was killing all the vegetation on the Romanian side of the Danube.

Not that higher lifestyles were unknown. At the Writers' Union, we had elegant snacks; every meeting began and ended with superb vodka and coffee. We ate in the state officials' dining room— formerly the Russian officers' club—where I had my first chicken Kiev, slivovitz, and the best white wine I had ever tasted—

Evxinograd (from the region of Homer's Euxine River).

Throughout the country, I was an object of curiosity. I had a beard—until very recently, illegal for all but priests. Now people tried to guess whether I was a priest, a foreigner, or a rebel; on the streets they stared openly. I encountered only one other beard—at the famous monastery of Rila. It is a beautiful site, high in the terribly abrupt mountains, its buildings made of alternating black and white blocks so that, at any distance, the buildings seemed striped. Our guide was a young priest, probably under thirty, his immaculate red beard trimmed and shaped. I could not help wondering if such care for personal appearance was proper for priests.

Part of the monastery now operated as an inn, another part as a museum. Our red-bearded guide took us from building to building pointing out a splendid collection of icons, paintings, religious sculptures, and artifacts. Each he identified, if possible, by its maker, place and date of making, special events in its history. The grand finale for this tour was an immense and ornate monstrance of gold and enamel work, set climactically on a table by itself. Noting its place and date of manufacture, he continued, "And here in the central glass bead is an actual piece of the True Cross. First century!" Could that be a joke?

Elsewhere, my beard marked me as a foreigner—but of a different background. When we visited Plovdiv (birthplace of Alexander the Great), the USIS man, knowing my interest in folk music, took me one evening to one of their cellar taverns that branch out in many directions like brick-lined mazes or catacombs. A gadulka player and a famous singer were scheduled to perform that evening, so the place was crowded; we shared a table with a Bulgarian laborer. Having had an appreciable start on us in alcohol, he seemed intent on increasing his lead. Sadly, drunks seem to spot me blocks away and will accept no substitute. Soon this one had pulled his stool next to mine, clamped his arm around my shoulders and was calling me "Ivan." He had decided I was a Russian friend who had worked with him on a gigantic dam in the USSR. When I told him that I was an American poet, he roared with laughter. "Come on, Ivan," he bellowed (in Bulgarian, of course), pounding me on the back, "how come you shit me like that?" Since he was bigger and would clearly be incensed if I were *not* Ivan, my guide and I finally confessed that's who I *was*, bought him several drinks and slipped away to the men's room.

Later, one of my hosts arranged for me to meet musician Philip Koutov (many of whose recordings became available in this country) and to attend one of his folklore ensemble's concerts. Koutov was delighted to find I was from Detroit: "Do you know where we learn Bulgarian dances? We send someone to Detroit! They've kept many of the dances better than we have here!"

The concert, it turned out, was in one of Sofia's suburbs. Through the smoke-filled dusk, our long official car edged away from the impressive buildings of the city center, through thousands of home-bound bicyclists, out to an area where the world seemed composed of vast, dimly lit, barracks-like buildings. "This is where most of the workers really live," I was told. At the huge auditorium everything had a curious expectancy which I supposed was in anticipation of the concert. My host, though, was disquieted and went off to ask questions, then came back to tell me, "We've got to leave."

Back in the car, he explained, "Those people in the front row are Vietnamese. Before the concert, they're going to hold a big rally. They'll say a lot of terrible things about the U.S., and I would have to get up and walk out. That would make a very bad scene." Back at the mission, the chief sympathized with our loss of the concert. I said I'd been involved at home in a number (perhaps inflated to salve my conscience) of demonstrations against our policy, but it seemed different to get involved there. "That's true," he grinned; "have a couple extras on us when you get back."

When it came time to leave for Romania, the mission supplied me with a compartment in a tidy, ancient train. They said we would reach the border during the night and that a border guard would come into the compartment and ask for my passport. I was to call them if anything went wrong—a frightening reassurance. In fact, I proved more frightening to the guard than he to me. When he appeared, I sat up in my bunk, held out my passport and said, "I'm sorry; I can only speak English." His mouth and eyes flew open; he shrieked, "EEEEngleeesh!" and vanished, slamming the compartment door. He never came back. He must have determined that no matter what he did, he would be in deep trouble. The only safe course was not to have seen me there at all.

* * *

Romania was utterly and instantly different. The Bulgarians, as I've noted had been all-Slav; the Romanians were busy being Romans. You certainly had no trouble seeing them—they were all out in the middle of the streets, arguing, bargaining, flirting. Ten years later, I went back; the Stalinist gray clothes I had seen had all turned gaudy—Carnaby St. outfits walked beside native folk embroideries. But they were still arguing, politicking, chattering. Only the Greeks, perhaps, do this with more dedication. This must be part of the national obsession that they are *really* Mediterraneans— the descendants of the native Dacians and the conquering Romans. That is the message of Hadrian's famous pillar—a copy of which they had made and brought to Bucharest. Yet, despite their Latin tongue (theirs is closest of all modern languages to ancient Latin), it is probable that they are the descendants of a Germanic tribe that moved in much later. But don't tell them that. A brave people who have had to be wily, they inhabit a region rich in soil, in oil, in mineral riches. A rhyming verse by the poet Octavian Goga says,

> Our hills are loaded with gold ore;
> Still we beg from door to door.

They have been systematically plundered by larger, powerful neighbors—Russians, Turks, Austrians, Hungarians, Germans— then by such of their own as Ceaușescu. (Incidentally, when the verse above was first quoted to me, it was identified as a "medieval folk poem"—the Communists could admit to neither the country's poverty nor their hand in causing it.) The Romanians, in any case, need a lineage to boost their confidence.

Unlike the Bulgarians, they hated and feared the Russians. Years later, my present wife and I spent weeks photographing a graveyard in a village just a mile from the border with what was then Ukraine—under Soviet domination and full of Russian troops. When that border had first been drawn, many in our village were separated from families and friends on the other side; every Sunday, they climbed nearby hills to shout across the no-man's-land (mined and machine-gun-guarded) to their grandparents, aunts and uncles, cousins. Every weekday, large truckloads of Romanian soldiers passed by, rowdy, rollicking, singing and cheering as they came off guard duty on that border. If the Russians ever *had* come across, not only those soldiers but most of our friends, writers and intellectuals, would have been wiped out—just as Ukrainian intellectuals had been annihilated in an earlier generation.

Like the Bulgarians, the Romanians paid constant praise to communism; unlike them, they paid no other service. Perhaps not wishing the Russians to think them "soft on capitalism," they maintained a constant but highly ineffective cloak-and-dagger air. Just outside your hotel, black marketeers offered to buy your hard currency at twice the official rate. The cultural attaché warned me that many of these were *securitate* agents who would arrest me and make a bad scene for the embassy.

If you left any city for a time, then returned, you were always given the same room in the same hotel—*it* had the *English* bug. Entering the room, we always praised the Romanian countryside and especially the diligence of our Romanian guides. One trip, I carried along a small lute so I could play through folk melodies and practice my fingering. Pity the poor *securitate* man who sat all those hours listening to my butterfingered playing and endless curses about it. If you went into a restaurant or bar—before Ceauşescu, some were splendid—within five minutes a solitary man wearing a hat took a seat at the nearest table to yours. "It's nothing personal, Snodders," said my Scottish friend, Roy MacGregor-Hastie, "he's just doing a job. If he orders a beer, you know he's a sergeant; if he orders a hard drink, you're getting up in the world—he's a lieutenant!"

The American cultural officer was both well-educated and savvy, qualities you could not take for granted. Giving me a tour of the small stone mansion where he lived, he showed me his wife's bedroom—larger than three normal-sized rooms—with its attached bath and dressing complex. "This is the room," he said, stirring every lurid fantasy in my mind, "where we ruined our image across all of Europe. The house was built by a rich Romanian for his French mistress." (Every Romanian male's fantasies involve a French love affair.) "This whole ceiling was covered with mirrors. When the embassy bought the place, they took them out. After I got here, the first thing *I* did was try to buy them back. Everyone in the city knew about them; no one would say where they'd gone."

Working at that time in the American embassy was a Romanian named Alexandru Ivasiuc, a small, dark man, scruffily dressed. A novelist who had served at least four years in prison because of his excellent early writings, he was one of the keenest-witted men I ever met. I was surprised that, now released, he would dare work for the Americans. I should have realized that this was precisely the point—his way back into favor with his own government meant working as their agent.

"You've noticed," he said, "how the younger generation stares at you in the street?" I nodded, though I'd noticed nothing of the sort—everyone had been generous and friendly to me. "You probably think that as Communists they disapprove of your luxuries. Don't believe it. They simply want your car. They want your coat."

Many years later, I returned to the Bucharest Writers' Union to have lunch with my friend and translator, Radu Lupan—the Union secretary who'd been so fiercely caricatured by Updike. Lupan pointed out, among a loud and boozy group at a corner table, Nichita Stanescu—whom they thought their greatest poet; I myself preferred Marin Sorescu. Out of that jovial group, one caught my eye, got up and came to our table. "Mr. Snodgrass?" he asked. "You don't recognize *me*, though, do you? That's because I look so fat and affluent since the last time we met." It was Ivasiuc, at least fifty pounds heavier and wearing an expensive, well-tailored suit. "I didn't look nearly so prosperous working for the capitalists, did I?" What he'd said about the young people may have had its truth—our beliefs usually have less command than our desires—but he'd surely told me more about himself. Moving rapidly upward through governmental circles, he was now himself the censor, sending other writers to prison. In 1977, during the terrible earthquake that struck

Bucharest, an apartment building collapsed; he was crushed in the street. Nothing less, I thought, could have halted that man's rise toward power.

My first visit fell just at Christmas, then called "Winter Holiday"—Christian terms were taboo. The man in the central square who wore a false beard, a red suit with white fur trim and who handed out gifts to children from his reindeer-drawn sleigh was not Santa Claus, but Father Winter. (As if Santa Claus had anything to do with Christianity, either in origin or results!) Because of the season, however, the poets, like migrant songbirds, were on vacation. I visited the Writers' Union; the few writers present were, like our cultural attaché, apologetic that I could not meet this or that important poet. It was hard to convince them that I did not *especially* want to meet poets. Experiences with Auden, with Frost, had convinced me that love for a poet's work might not make that person likable. Worse, because of the language difficulties, we might be unable to discuss the one thing foremost in our minds: poetry. I would about as soon meet truck drivers, I said. Was there no one, they persevered, I specially wanted to meet? Well, when I thought it over, yes: musicians, especially those involved with early music and/or folk music.

That meant, said the cultural attaché, that I should visit the splendid Folklore Institute—folklore is of immense importance to Romanians. In this, though, he couldn't help me. The embassy could apply for permission, but official channels would take ages. Even if permission ever came through, I'd have been gone for months by then. He suggested that I should just go to the Folklore Institute, several blocks away, walk in and tell them who I was and what I wanted—seemingly unaware of official channels or of his advice.

It took me several days to gather nerve. The lady who met me at the door may not have understood a word I said, but after a few minutes, she ushered me into a central office. There I was greeted, in perfect English, by the very distinguished (as I later learned) ethno-musicologist, Dr. Mihai Pop (pronounced "Pope"). An hour later, I emerged laden with books, offprints of essays, phonograph records. Among these was a performance by a peasant, Alexandru

Cercel, of a ballad called "Mioritsa" or "The Ewe Lamb." Unknown elsewhere in Europe, it is familiar to every Romanian. Streets, magazines, and gift shops are named after it, every singer knows at least one melody for it, every literary critic has at least one essay about it. Listening to Cercel's marvelous singing without any least notion of what he was singing about, I knew that I had to make a singable translation of it.

Though I eventually translated five of the Romanian ballads, it was largely because of this one magnificent song that I received a medal from what may well have been the worst government then in the world. Years after these events—I had visited Romania a number of times between—I received an invitation to a translators' conference in Bucharest. Since I wouldn't understand the meetings (I don't speak or read Romanian) and couldn't afford the air fare, I had regretfully declined. Then I received a phone call from the Romanian Embassy in Washington urging me to go. The cable from Bucharest, I was told, was somewhat scrambled, but it appeared that I was to receive a Medal for Cultural Achievement.

That, of course, changed everything. I could now apply to Syracuse University, where I taught, for travel funds. The grant came through and I went; though I didn't understand the meetings, I loved seeing the city and several old friends, among them Radu Lupan as well as Ioan Popa, who had published a book of his translations of my poems. Still, no one said a word about a medal.

A day or two before I was to leave, I asked Radu Lupan when the medal was to be awarded. He looked astonished: "What medal?" Going off to inquire, he came back with the news that no one had heard anything about medals. That *was* a problem: I couldn't afford to repay the $1,000 air fare. I came up with a solution. "Could you write me a letter in Romanian? It doesn't matter what it says so long as it looks very official and has a lot of governmental stamps or seals." The next day he handed me just such a letter, assuring me that it said I was to receive my medal at a later date.

Strangely, when I returned home no one at the University even asked about the medal; I soon forgot the whole matter. But roughly six months later, I got another call from the Romanian embassy, asking me to come to Buffalo on a certain date so that the Romanian

Ambassador, who would be visiting the city, could present my medal. Unfortunately, I had arranged, many months before, to give a poetry reading on that date; it could not be postponed. Several weeks later, in the rural mailbox some quarter mile from our backwoods farmhouse near Erieville, New York, a plain cardboard box appeared. Inside, heavy bronze and large as a tea saucer, was a Romanian Centennial Medal—usually awarded for military prowess, a field in which I scarcely excel.

On my next visit to Bucharest, I was eager to tell Radu Lupan about this. Noticing the *securitate* man at the next table, we took a walk in the park while I recounted my medal's absurd history. "You think that's funny?" he laughed. "Everyone at that conference had been promised a medal; that's why they were all here. *You* actually got one because we'd written you a letter about it."

* * *

One of the ethnic jokes going the rounds in the U.S. at that time warned: "If you go into a revolving door ahead of a Hungarian, you'll come out behind him." In the Budapest train station, I devised a new version: "If you get into a taxi queue behind Hungarians, you'll never pay a taxi fare." Someone was always jumping the line, pushing, shouting, disputing their position. Inside the city, one evening, after waiting at least an hour, I finally got a cab only to have two plainclothes policemen rush up, flash their badges, and commandeer it for themselves.

Throughout the city, buildings showed damage so extensive that I supposed it had happened while they were driving out the Nazis at the end of World War II; it had actually been done by the Russians during the uprising of 1956. I gathered from Hungarian friends that the Soviet tanks had blasted buildings at random, regardless of any sign of hostile fire or intent. Yet no one evinced any specific feeling about either the Russians or communism—or about the Americans who had encouraged their revolt, then gave them no support. Meantime, Cardinal Mindszenti was still living on an upper floor of our embassy; for everyone else, it seemed to be each man for himself.

A similarly guarded air hung over my visit to the Writers' Union. Earlier, in Sofia, I had been asked to summarize recent literary trends in America; having done so, I had asked for a similar summary about Bulgaria. The answer, by the Union's president— a small man who looked as if he might be a baker or plumber— while never departing from a possible Communist agenda, forthrightly laid out a series of movements and disagreements that had arisen within the Union since World War II.

Trying the same approach in Budapest, I asked about recent literary movements. At once, one of the writers arose to say, "Gentlemen, I propose a toast to Brotherhood in the Arts." I could not believe my ears. I drank the toast, made a few remarks about my own literary history, then rephrased my question. Again, one of the writers rose to toast some indisputable virtue. Downing another glass of *barack pálinka* (splendid apricot brandy), I realized that one more such question might stretch me under the table. I later learned there had been a recent reshuffling inside the Union—no doubt related to the anti-Soviet revolt and its bloody end. The Union's current president, Ivan Boldizsar, had been in prison four different times. Though many poets of deserved renown were there, it seemed clear I would never know their opinions on either poetry or politics.

Again, I took refuge among musicologists. Friends sent me to the eminent Bence Szabolcsi. A cheerful, frail gnome of a man, he graciously received me at his apartment and began at once to outline the far-Eastern sources of Hungarian melody; he had traced the eighth-century invasions through the history of songs. At the piano, he played first Hungarian, then Mongolian tunes, asking if they weren't the same melodies, then pointing to his cheekbones to exclaim gleefully, "You see? We're really Tartars!"

By the time of my next visit to Hungary, he had died. The same friends suggested that I contact Lajos Vargyas who was director of the state folk music archives, the depository of those collections made by Bartók, Kodály, and their colleagues. He, too, greeted me eagerly, making an appointment to see me the very next day. He was, however, blunt in rejecting the high-toned translation I had already made of one Hungarian ballad, "The Little Yellow Snake."

He explained that ballads were, after all, a peasant art form; while their language was removed and formalized from normal conversation, the result had no relation to any high "literary" style. Fortunately, that night I was able to recast the ballad's language; having seen that, he felt we could work together.

Even here, I found a curious wariness. I began by asking Dr. Vargyas which, among the Hungarian ballads, was his favorite—not realizing that most folklorists think it improper to prefer one ballad to another, or even to discuss a song's aesthetic qualities. In reply, he quoted Bartók to the effect that every Hungarian ballad was a shining masterpiece. Our situation was much like that at the Writers' Union; the archive was, after all, state-controlled and even to express an opinion at odds with Bartók's was unthinkable heresy.

Determined not to be put off again, I devised a kind of ritual question-and-answer game. Agreeing with Bartók's statement, I went on to ask, "If, however, at some time, this building were to catch fire and you only had time to save one manuscript, which one would you snatch up?" He replied, at once, "'Barcsai.'" "Fine," I said. "Could we look at a version of it?" "Which version do you want?" he asked. "Which is the best?" I answered, inadvertently restarting the ritual. "Every single one is an unmatched masterpiece," he retorted. So I recounted how my teacher, Randall Jarrell, when he went into the Army, had typed two poems of Hardy's on tissue paper, then hid them in the lining of his wallet. "If you were drafted tomorrow, which version of 'Barcsai' would you hide in your wallet?" "Why, this one," he said, opening a file drawer and handing me a paper from a folder. "Look," he said, "that's Bartók's writing." I stared, then quickly moved my coffee cup farther off. "Now," I said (skipping the first steps of the dance), "if you were printing a new book on Hungarian ballads and had room for only one 'Barcsai' melody, which would you use?" "Probably this one," he replied, opening another drawer, but then turned to a second folder, "although *this* is easier for Westerners to sing." We sat down with these materials and he made for me, line by line, a literal translation of that fierce song.

This was our pattern, day after day. Each night, back at my apartment, I silently rehearsed all the different emergencies which might arise and force him to rescue one ballad, one version, one melody, abandoning the others. Each day he sat with me, explaining, translating, singing. A magical time.

Meantime, Ivan Boldizsar, the president of the Writers' Union who'd earlier been so cagey, turned out to be a fine companion— surprisingly open when away from other writers. He not only took me to the best and most famous restaurants and bars; he introduced me to chicken paprikas, chocolate palacintas, to the red wines and Tokay. One day, having led me to a *Bizományi* (a resale shop where once-wealthy families sold antiques and heirlooms), he approached with a twinkle in his eye to ask, "Is there a lady in the case?" When I avowed that one might possibly be found, he led me into a cluttered back room. There, in an obscure and half-covered cabinet, lay two of the fabulous sword-belts that Hungarian nobles had once worn. Both were made of heavily gilded silver links and had three large bosses set with turquoise and coral. The less ornate—and less expensive—cost $250. My Scottish ancestors trembled at this, but I bought it for my ladyfriend. I should have bought both—when I had some small repairs made in the States, the jeweler offered me five times the amount I'd paid.

Sadly, however hard I tried, I could not make singable translations of the marvelous old-style ballads. In Hungarian, every single word is accented on the first syllable. In these ballads, sung without accompaniment and (like the Scots ballads) without expressive style, musical accent and language stress often conflict; otherwise, the rhythm would be deadly boring. Vargyas himself sang to show how folksingers could juggle and balance out these competing emphases. (Strangely enough, singers of Romanian—like English, a language with variable stresses—also learn to do this.) To ask this of singers trained in English, where stress is so distinctive and powerful, would be senseless. Moreover, I also was used to our linkage of stress and accent, and couldn't separate them meaningfully.

Instead, I made singable translations of quite a few lighter folk songs and, back in the U.S., collected these into a small book, superbly printed with a decorative design by Charles Seluzicki, a private publisher. Ironically, this book's beauty made it so costly that neither poets nor folksingers would ever see it; almost every copy went to collectors who cared only about the quality of the paper and the printing.

From my Romanian visits, I also managed to translate many folk songs but was never able to obtain the music for them, so could not make them singable. As noted before, I did manage five of their greatest ballads; though almost unknown in the West, the originals are true masterpieces. These, too, were published, with authentic melodies, in a tidy little inexpensive volume. But this is found only in Romania, where anyone who wants to sing a ballad would sing in Romanian. I am almost the only one who ever sees this book in the U.S. and, worse, there is so much Eastern and Turkish influence in the melodies that I seldom sing them myself. It's a style that you have to take in with your mother's milk. Don't ask, then, why I made such translations. Perhaps because the only real reason to try to translate any song (or even a poem, for that matter) is that it can't be done. As Koz'ma Prutkov, the famous Russian hoax-poet had warned, you may not be able to compass the unencompassable. But if you should even come close, you will feel like a god among mortals.

So I brought away from my Balkan visits not only a taste for strange food and drink, but these three small books: *Traditional Hungarian Songs, Star and Other Poems*, by Eminescu, and *Five Romanian Ballads*; I feel grateful to those who sent me there. There was one book I didn't bring away. Besides the Hungarian folk songs, I also discovered an early singer, Tinodi Sebestyén, known as Tinodi the Lutenist, who sang for patrons at his wife's wine shop in the village of Kassa. Among his songs is a book-length chronicle about the battle against the Turks at nearby Eger in 1552, a book which every Hungarian school child once read and which has a delicious, naive clumsiness somewhat like that of Scotland's McGonagall. On a later visit to Hungary, I was able to do not only a sizable chunk of Tinodi's chronicle but also his hilarious song about the many kinds of drunkards found in Hungary. That song ends by thanking God they'd beaten those puritans, the Turks—otherwise he'd have had to drink water till reeds grew out of his nose! (He never mentions that only a year later the Turks came back and easily captured the town.)

To translate these songs (I don't read Hungarian, either), I worked with a woman assigned by the Writers' Union and, as no complete edition of Tinodi is available there, I had brought one made in Canada. When I came to leave the country I found that she hadn't returned this book and, though I tried many avenues of recovery, never saw it again.

There is another ethnic joke which circulates only in the Balkans. It always involves three cities though these will vary according to where you hear the story; in the version I heard a ghost appeared one night in the streets of Sofia, carrying a lantern. Ordered by a militiaman to halt, show its identity card and state its name and business, it replied, "I am the ghost of Diogenes and I'm looking for an honest man." The militiaman, terrified that he'd get into trouble, told it to clear out. Two weeks later, it appeared in Bucharest and, challenged, made the same avowal. Two weeks later still, it appeared in Budapest and when stopped and challenged, answered the militiaman, "I am the ghost of Diogenes and I'm looking for my lantern."

Leaving the country and asked for my passport, I wished I dared reply, "I am the ghost of Tinodi the Lutenist and I'm looking for my songbook."

✦

XI. THE BATTLE OF THE BUNKER

After my disastrous playwriting class at the University of Iowa, any sensible person would surely have found something else to write about. And I did try several other subjects. With one of my students, I wrote a full-length play about the modeling school in Detroit where she had worked. I tried a play about Elvis Presley's hitch in the Army. I translated *Biedermann and the Firebugs*, by Max Frisch, but, as I noted earlier, could not get permission for either publication or performance.

If I asked myself why my first book of poems had "succeeded," it seemed I'd taken a subject no one else had broached in poetry—the loss of children in a divorce. If I asked what important subject our poetry was now ignoring, the answer seemed obvious: the Nazis. At the same time, everyone (except poets) *was* writing about them—during the next twenty years, more books appeared about them than any other subject, possibly excluding cooking and its attendant twin, dieting. They all found buyers: memoirs of statesmen, rulers, generals, diplomats on both sides, long-distance psychoanalyses, histories and biographies, books on particular battles, analyses of strategic blunders, picture books of the whole war, of German tanks and planes, insignia and battle gear. Innumerable television documentaries and several movies, one starring Alec Guinness, appeared.

Of course, vice has always held more fascination than virtue: as Freud noted, why make all those rules *against* evil if evil weren't terribly attractive? Who reads either *Paradiso* or *Purgatorio*? Twice? We read Satan's speeches in *Paradise Lost*, not God's. What actor wouldn't rather play Iago than Othello? Edmund rather than Albany? If Hardy could write a play about Napoleon only a century after the British had defeated him, and Aeschylus one about Xerxes and Darius only eighteen years after helping defeat them at Marathon, why not take those examples?

I may have overlooked, though, a special factor. Surely a sense of guilt and fright lay behind much of this craving for publications about the Third Reich. We had destroyed Dresden and hundreds of thousands of civilians to no military purpose; we had dropped the atom bomb—which could now be dropped on us. As never before, we needed to focus on the crimes of others. My attitude, as I returned to the material again and again, was much like everyone else's: how could *those* people have done those things?

Two moments—both, oddly enough, onstage—suggested I should continue. The first was at a discussion of current American poetry in a New York television station. The panel was chaired by Heywood Hale Broun, Jr., and included Allen Ginsberg and Amiri Baraka. I had already met Ginsberg; I was introduced to Baraka at the studio where I congratulated him on his play *Dutchman* which I'd seen the night before. His answer was surly—partly, I assume, because I was with a young black woman whom I had known in Detroit and had encountered again in New York. He had a white wife; I hadn't supposed he would resent my dating a black woman.

This was in the heyday of the widely touted split in American poetry between "beat" and "academic" poets. The panel started with Ginsberg and Baraka denouncing most American poetry as timid, academic, complicit with the evils of the military-industrial complex. Broun, smaller and softer of voice than his famous father, asked what was so evil about American poetry. Baraka pointed at me and said, "He is!" As he repeated this, Ginsberg and several others joined in. In moments, they all seemed to be circling me like a wolf pack, declaiming the wickedness of myself and my writing. I was too astonished to say anything and Broun called an intermission.

Sylvia, the young black woman who'd come there with me, pulled me aside to say, "Don't you try to answer them. They don't care what they say. They're like street kids: they'll just shout you down and make you look weak or foolish." Perhaps I should have listened. Instead, when we started up again, I thanked them for what I took for a compliment. Though I doubted that I really *had* managed to contain, or express, the evils of America (or of any empire), nonetheless a poetry that even appeared to do that must be very broad and powerful and I was glad for their appreciation; I could only wish they were right. Later, I came to realize that my smart-alecky answer (which *did* surprise and quiet them) had some truth to it.

The second event took place during an arts conference at Duke University. The participants were the cartoonist-playwright, Jules Feiffer, novelist Ralph Ellison, theater director Allan Schneider, and myself; the moderator was Thomas Driver, a critic. He and Ellison began by discussing the identification with evil often found in art; this came to focus on the figure of Madame Nhu who had recently been driven out of Vietnam. She indeed seemed wickedly tyrannical, but before long I heard Ellison following his own thoughts into surprising areas. Though he had always detested her and her policies, he said, when he seriously thought about it, he couldn't be sure, if he had been in her place—raised a strict Catholic, seeing herself and her family as representatives of divine order on earth—that he wouldn't have made many of the same decisions. He hoped, of course, that he would have been more reasonable and humane in executing a policy, but he couldn't honestly say he was sure. This suggested to him that there might be a positive value, a self-recognition in that identification with evil which art may offer. I found this a marvelously decent and (ironically) humane statement—just what I'd have expected from Ellison. I am not a Christian but felt I had finally met one—a man who could admit that his enemies' evils were, at least in part, at least potentially, his own.

For a time, I actually tried to change the subject of my work to Madame Nhu. I had recently heard a gamelan orchestra for the first time and thought that it, or related Oriental music, would make a marvelous background for a staged drama. Alas, I could not learn enough about her or her family to put together a drama. Perhaps our news had been manipulated until the true facts were lost; perhaps the American public simply lost interest and didn't care. Probably both were true and played into each other's hands. From the point of view of my work, it may be just as well: where could we ever find gamelan players for a stage performance?

After many years—perhaps around 1970—when I was teaching in Syracuse, I read Albert Speer's *Inside the Third Reich* and decided to try a monologue in his voice. At that time, we had little information about Speer beyond his own writings and I had to guess at any guilts beyond those he reveals. Though parts of his book seemed suspect, much else seemed (and still does) straightforward; he at least seemed less vile than most of that regime. To my surprise, when I read this monologue to friends, they were pleased. I began to wonder if a series of monologues mightn't be the form I'd been looking for. That could give me another cycle, a long poem made up of shorter ones.

Gradually, the idea emerged that each figure might have his or her own characteristic verse form. First, Speer's poem broke into three separate poems, each as long as the original had been. Then I tried casting his poems into triangular stanzas in which lines would grow progressively longer until a pyramid had been formed, whereon a new pyramid could begin. This might reflect the bunker steps which, in poem after poem, Speer was climbing or descending. It seemed also to reflect his (and Hitler's) obsession with size and growth, as well as Speer's large personal size. More, it yielded a form where the line had no relation to sound, to any rhythm or music in the voice—related, I felt, to a crucial lack of mental or emotional richness that underlay Speer's willingness to blind himself to what was going on—a rigid order based entirely on the conscious will and cut off from the richer musics of the unconscious.

In 1972, on a Guggenheim fellowship, I was able to visit Germany and to interview Speer. Released from Spandau for some years, he now lived in his family's home just above the castle in Heidelberg. His nearest neighbor was the American commanding general of all NATO forces. When I remarked on this anomaly, he spoke of people's stares when he recently had lunch in Vienna with Simon Wiesenthal whom, he implied, he was helping to track down escaped Nazi criminals. Of course, by now, such writers as Matthias Schmidt have made clear the extent of Speer's criminal involvements. But just as Gitta Sereny (who was fully aware of his guilts) has pictured him, Speer was personable, courteous, intelligent, anxious to condemn the Nazi regime, but thereby to clear himself. Certainly, the breast-beating I'd found so questionable in *The Spandau Diaries* was absent.

I explained that a part of my fascination with the last days in the bunker was the intensity of betrayals being plotted on all sides there. Speer had written, I noted, that merely by joining the Nazi Party he had betrayed his family's liberal ideals. He agreed, but added that he had been an ambitious young architect and in his depressed country could build nothing; suddenly he'd been given the chance to build everything. "I don't think even my father," he said, "could have resisted that temptation." That, I felt, was the real man talking—assenting to the accusation, yet forgiving himself through the imagined example of his father, who'd always seemed to him the epitome of rectitude.

I asked about Hitler's motives in ordering more and more counterattacks in those last days when the war was clearly lost—as Hitler had known for perhaps two years. What could that serve except to cause more casualties which Hitler could interpret as sacrifices made to him and inflating his figure in history (a motive previously suggested, I believe, only by the playwright Ionesco). At once, Speer stated that we could not know about any motive beyond the conscious purposes a person acknowledges. Pursuing this, I asked how Hitler could order out units everyone else knew were in ruins, men who were dead. Speer answered that Hitler had been like a doctor he'd known, a cancer specialist who could merely look at a patient and tell whether they had cancer; the doctor had, besides, predicted that he himself would die of cancer, yet when he fell victim, he alone did not know. "He neglected his knowing," Speer said in his slightly unorthodox English. That self-deception seemed so central, so crucial not only to Hitler, but to Speer as well, that I formed another poem around his sentence.

As our talk was finishing, Speer's little granddaughter ran into the room and leaped on the couch where she bounced up and down in her stocking feet. She spoke perfect English. When I asked about this, Speer said that his son was teaching in Chicago, where he had recently visited and where she had grown up. The ironies seemed endless.

Since the triangulated shapes appeared to work for Speer's poems, it seemed reasonable to try similar forms for the other characters. For Himmler, head of the SS and Gestapo, probably the most vile of all, I devised the most rigidly arbitrary form possible: capital letters printed on graph paper, thirty letters and spaces to the line, with an alphabet acrostic (omitting "X") down the left-hand margin. I called this form the "platoon"; on the page it breaks into five "squads" of five lines each. There is no indication where sentences begin and end, so adding to the tonelessness of this "idealistic" weakling and fuddy-duddy who administered the murder of millions.

For Goebbels, I chose rhyming tetrameter couplets, thinking (mistakenly) that this was the form of Mephistopheles' speeches in Goethe's *Faust*. Later, I was chagrined to find that Mephistopheles actually uses longer and looser lines. But these short, tight couplets seemed right for a person partially malformed and so (like Pope) obsessed with the minutiae of forms. For Goebbels' wife, Magda, who had always traded on her beauty and had been notably unfaithful to those who loved her, I chose the fancier French love forms—rondels, triolets, villanelles, etc. The repetition and seductive guile of such poems seemed like that of Nazi (or any other) propaganda; if it's the truth, you say it once.

Free verse seemed more appropriate for other characters. Martin Bormann's poems contrast his mushy love letters to his wife against his personal machinations to usurp power. Eva Braun's poems often concern snapshots she actually took, trying to substantiate her life and her ties to Hitler but constantly offset by songs or religious music which point toward her less conscious thoughts. Hitler's poems pit his thoughts about the battlefront situation against recollections and quotations from his past, their indentation showing how far back these memories reach. These aim to show the virulence of his lifelong hunger for power and consequent rage to destroy anything beyond his control.

This process, of course, took many years. Meantime, even though some of these poems were published in magazines and journals, critics complained that I had not written anything in years. When I visited the State University of New York's Brockport campus for a reading and an interview with Al Poulin and Bill Heyen, I was pleased by their interest in the cycle. Poulin was starting a small press, BOA Editions, and planning a series which would couple an offbeat volume by an established poet with one by a younger poet of his/her choosing. I thought my student, Barton Sutter, should be published, so I offered Poulin a selection from my cycle together with Sutter's first book, *Cedarhome*. These appeared in handsome editions in 1977, the first pairing in BOA's new list. My book was titled *The Führer Bunker: A Cycle of Poems in Progress*. Poulin and I met in the Rochester, NY, airport bar—I was en route to a reading elsewhere—and in about four hours we completed the editing. Meantime, we each drank six or eight strong martinis—the tension so high that neither felt the least effect. Not that we were combative; he was an ideal editor (earlier, I'd also had the good luck to have Fran McCullough), full of ideas but willing to cede when I could not agree.

Foolishly, I thought this book would *quiet* criticism! Most scholarly sources now say that the book provoked a storm of controversy; that's not true, either. Roughly a third of the reviewers were friendly and impressed; more were unfavorable in a hesitant, slightly puzzled way. Hugh Kenner was openly hostile, saying that I could not know what these characters thought or felt and that I should find worthier subjects. My favorite review said, "I don't think I'm ready for this." I thought: great; read it again in ten years. Fifty would have been likelier.

In fact, the book was picked for, but did not receive, the National Book Critics Circle Award in 1978. One of the judges later told me they had agreed to give my book the award, but before this was announced, Robert Lowell had died—so they gave it to *Day by Day*, which I thought not up to his best work. One year before, this prize had been created specifically because the other awards—the Pulitzer and the National Book Award—had been given so often, for nonliterary considerations, to inferior books. Some author, perhaps, had been passed over for an earlier award he or she deserved, or because they were in great hardship, or had been picked because of some temporary fashion. This new award was to be given strictly to the best book in its category that year—now, its second time around, the principle had been broken.

The ironies of my relation to Lowell were continuing. He had at first rejected my *Heart's Needle* but changed his mind several years later; then he had not only found my book a publisher, but had scared me blue by writing to say he was taking those poems as a model. In no time, though, critical doctrine held that I had followed him in such subjects. Later, he had written that I was hated in some circles because of this newer cycle, but that he wanted to be counted among its supporters. Shortly before his death he wrote again to say, "I have been haunted by your Hitler. . . . Having tried a few short pieces on Hitler myself, I would have thought your undertaking impossible. You should be very proud."

I was already deeply grateful to him; I was more than proud of his support and good opinion. And shocked when his death deprived us all of an astonishing sensibility, deprived me of an irreplaceable friend and, at the same stroke, of that award which might have profoundly affected the reception of my work.

If there was little open acrimony, there *was* a growing sense of unspoken accusation and resentment. I first discovered this when reading at the University of Pennsylvania for Stephen Berg, who'd published several sections in *The American Poetry Review*. In the discussion afterward, a man got up to shout, "How dare you glorify these monsters," talking at length about their obvious crimes and atrocities. Fortunately, the audience rose to point out, from the poems themselves, that the Nazis had not been glorified but rather depicted as fearfully evil. I went home feeling justified and pleased. A few days later, I got a letter from the same man, repeating his earlier accusations with a single change: not that I had "glorified" but that I had "humanized" the Nazis.

This has been a common charge. I have sometimes regretted that, as an atheist, I couldn't reply that you can't blame me for God's doing. What I did say was that one of the chief Nazi crimes was to deny humanity to the Jews; that gave us no right to deny theirs. Or to adopt any other of their practices. I doubt that this changed his mind; his attitude was fixed and typical of others since. People recognize that the poems won't support any accusation of Nazi sympathies. Yet they feel threatened, themselves accused by any admission that we too have committed shameful acts, that nothing human is foreign to us. In place of answerable accusations, there have been rumors, innuendos, and unspoken blame.

As my work continued, and as the world developed after the war, it got harder to avoid seeing that all the nations who had combined to defeat the Nazis were committing acts more than sufficiently Nazi-like. That picture only grew worse as one looked back through our histories. Winners, of course, write the history books, and most people take winning as a sign of virtue. The reverse may be truer; wars are seldom won by virtuous actions. Again, many feel that others' wickedness proves their own virtue; it seemed to me more often a clue to one's own potential. I had come to feel—no doubt echoing the Christian teachings of my childhood—that the only way to a better world was to recognize one's own faults and try to control them; there was surely little else in the world you could control.

The resentment was not a surprise—its longevity was. When I mentioned this once to Al Poulin, he simply said, "They'll never forgive you." Magazines which had once supported me now rejected everything coldly; I was no longer proposed for prestigious committees; my work appeared in fewer and fewer anthologies or critical appraisals. At first, I thought I was being paranoid about this, but more and more occasions demonstrated otherwise. From time to time, those who'd been on award committees told me how, when my name was proposed, another judge (I was never told who) would say, "That man will receive an award only over my dead body!" I told myself that *Heart's Needle* had also been disapproved at first but that people had swung around to it. Still, nothing good seemed to be swinging my way. Larry Levis, one of the few who had written strongly praising the poems already published, was asked to submit this to a collection of pieces about my work. Instead, he submitted a new essay describing how Gerald Stern had badgered him—"but they're Nazis, Larry, Nazis!"—until he had come to doubt the cycle's worth. Worse yet, Geoffrey Helterman, writing in the prestigious *Dictionary of Literary Biography*, supposedly paraphrasing a statement from my "Afterword," claimed "[Snodgrass] admits to making the Nazis more attractive than they were in life." I had said the opposite—that this depiction of the Nazis differed from their public appearance in that they spoke only within themselves and so could say things they never would have admitted in public.

I did not find this easy to live with. Some—e.g., certain athletes—thrive on dislike and public disapproval. I am not of that tribe; dislike, frankly, shakes me.

During this long process of composition, I had happened to run into Wynn Handman, the director of the American Place Theater in New York. Back in 1965, I'd met him at Lyndon Johnson's inauguration, then again when I'd reviewed Lowell's *The Old Glory*. Later, I had submitted a playscript to him which, fortunately, he'd chosen not to produce. Now, though, he said he'd like to see another play from me. When I replied that between the demands of my collapsing third marriage, of extra teaching and of preparing this new book, I'd have to postpone that, he suggested that I script a stage version of this cycle. On receiving the script of *The Führer Bunker*, he scheduled run-throughs, selecting a director, Carl Weber, who had worked with Bertolt Brecht in Berlin for ten years; together they chose a cast. We mounted three takes of this —three entirely different conceptions, settings, and styles. The audience, of course, saw only the last of these—a shame, I thought, since the second seemed far more exciting and projective of the text.

In our first mounting, the stage had a realistic setting, each role was taken by a single actor, the music (by the well-known stage composer Richard Peaslee) was melodic, chordal, and much like what they played in Berlin through the '30s or '40s At the first run-through, I was pleased—as were Wynn and Carl. Peaslee, though, objected that this setting did no real service to the text. This was not a play—it was more like an oratorio for speakers; Donald Hall once called it an opera. Such a staging would lead audiences to expect the kind of conflict and resolution found in standard dramas: they would surely be disappointed. Here, there could be little direct conflict between characters; Hitler, still alive, would squelch any open rebellion. Instead, the conflict lay within individual characters as they tried either to replace Hitler, to defeat each other, to escape or to justify their obvious guilts in the face of imminent defeat or capture.

The second mounting, some months later, seemed far better. Here, we used an open stage, placing a live percussionist and a synthesizer downstage between the audience and actors. Each role could be shared out to several actors. Microphones were buried onstage and speakers hidden around the auditorium. If several actors were onstage, you might not be sure which you were hearing—though the actor speaking might be downstage left, his voice might come from a speaker behind you. The music, again by Peaslee, was free-form and experimental—sometimes more like surreal sound effects than conventional music. We finished less than half this version before time ran out, but we did one run-through for anyone who happened to be in the building that day. We all thought it splendidly effective.

Months passed before the third mounting, which would go into production. As I was teaching then and my personal life was chaotic, I missed the first weeks' rehearsals. Several actors, expectably, had had to be replaced. To my astonishment, a whole new conception was also in place, bringing the piece back toward the realistic first version. Several small stages had been constructed at the sides and back of the auditorium; individual scenes now took place in these realistic settings. Each role had returned to a single actor or actress. The percussionist had been moved off to one side; the synthesizer had been replaced by an accordionist—a fine musician but far too realistic, I thought, too much like the historical '40s.

Besides, the director and the new designer had come up with distracting accoutrements: several cages of live white rabbits were placed conspicuously onstage; the floor between the audience and the downstage edge was filled by piles of debris, notably wrecked television sets. (This anachronism was meant to suggest that the rise of Nazism had been caused by the collapse of bourgeois morality; the rabbits apparently to portray the situation of Goebbels' children, called in the text, "poor trapped rabbits.")

Carl and Wynn could not be dissuaded; this was the show presented to audiences. Both agreed about the success of the second version, but felt that to continue the electronic amplification for so long a period would overstrain the audience. I am not sure what drastic action might have been open to me; it seemed better to trust their theatrical experience and see what came of it. I must say that as rehearsals progressed, I was fascinated to see how a group of excellent actors and this expert director worked together.

In one scene—among the most horrifying—Magda Goebbels (played by Catherine Byers) prepares to leave her estate on the Wannsee near Berlin, taking her six young children to the bunker where, when defeat is final, she will kill them. The problem was how to show that, leaving home, she plans never to return. Various props and actions—suitcases, dustcovers—seemed inadequate. Then Carl recalled that his aunt, who had lived in Berlin, had kept an end table in her living room with many framed photos of friends and relatives. Magda, determined to perform an act that horrifies even herself, went to the end table, picked up the photos of her children, then with one sweep of her arm crashed all the other photos to the floor. When she slammed the children's pictures face down into her open suitcase and slammed its cover shut, you could practically hear bones break.

As noted, the director, Carl, was German; the producer, Wynn, like two-thirds of the cast and crew, was Jewish—many of them dedicated to Jewish causes and aims. They certainly saw nothing in the text sympathetic to the Nazis and played their roles accordingly. Still, rehearsals and performances were replete with ironies and paradoxes. During the first mounting of the show, Carl had brought in an old record of a dirty German song, "Herr Bälle" (Mister Balls) to be played in one scene. When one of the actors asked why he had saved this record all these years, he replied, "Insurance against homesickness."

Perhaps the most memorable figure was Robert Stattel—an experienced actor who'd done many important classic and modern roles with off-Broadway groups. He was, of course, Jewish—his name derives from the Yiddish *shtetl*, meaning a Jewish village or settlement. Onstage, in uniform and wearing Hitler's infamous moustache, he simply exuded evil; offstage, he was the epitome of thoughtful, friendly cooperation. After one of the tense, exhausting, seemingly endless final days of tech and dress rehearsals, Stattel went home and baked cookies for the cast and crew.

When it came time to make final cuts, we faced a problem: Carl had already had several disputes with one actor about cutting certain lines of his. The actor hinted strongly that he might "walk" if those lines were taken. Feeling that the actors couldn't dictate such matters, I offered to announce the cuts. Stattel faced much more severe losses—besides playing Hitler, he had doubled as SS General Fegelein, a sleazy opportunist married to Eva Braun's younger sister. Caught sneaking out of Berlin, he had been brought back into the bunker in his underwear, roaring drunk, frog-marched through the sexual orgy that had broken out there, then up into the garden and shot.

I first announced that this scene would have to go. Stattel's good grace in losing a whole scene he loved to play cleared the way for others to accept cuts. For several days, the other man's playing was numb and lackluster, but Carl reassured me, "In front of an audience, he'll come alive." Carl knew actors; from opening night, the role was played brilliantly.

As for Stattel, the ironies of his situation scarcely escaped him. One day, during the scheduled run, water pipes burst and the dressing rooms were flooded. Backstage, the cast set up small makeup tables near their entrance points. That evening, having delivered a long speech in which Hitler triumphantly totals the death-count he has caused then commits suicide, Stattel stepped off the stage to his dressing table saying, "Somehow it seems you ought to have to go more than ten feet to get from Adolf Hitler to Bob Stattel!"

Every evening, after the performance, a discussion was held between the director, producer and audience. Not living in New York, I seldom attended these; they were said to be less controversial and rancorous than expected. The single evening I *was* there a considerable hullabaloo broke out. Among the first to speak was a young man, slight of build, dark and intense, who delivered a fierce diatribe. Claiming that the choruses (representing the common people of Berlin) demanded special sympathy for the Germans, he went on to say that he had been at Auschwitz and that these people deserved no sympathy; he hoped they'd all be wiped out. This provoked cheers and loud applause.

Wynn restrained me: "I have something to tell you later," he whispered urgently. I wanted to point out that the aim of these choruses was to highlight the astonishing loyalty of the citizens to leaders who showed no least loyalty to them. Rather than ask for special sympathy, the choruses had admitted that Berliners were suffering just what they had inflicted on others. Still, you could hardly ask them to be happy about the destruction raining down on them in air raids and artillery bombardments. Again, I thought it might not be a bad idea to feel some sympathy for those you were forced to injure or kill. Certain African tribes, after a war, ask their gods' forgiveness for those they've killed: it didn't seem that we should be less civilized. If we rejoiced in the indiscriminate slaughter and maiming of any and all enemy civilians, it didn't much matter who lost the war—the Nazis' values had won.

Wynn would let me say none of this, again saying he'd explain later. Soon, however, he turned the discussion to other subjects and other members of the audience. Among these was another young man, rather portly and sitting near the front; asked what he thought of the show, he replied, "I think it's monumental," going on to discuss, keenly, the work's intentions. The discussion turned to other matters and shortly broke up.

In the lobby, Wynn and I again encountered the first man, now haranguing a group on the same subject. Quickly, Wynn pulled me aside, whispering, "He's one of my students. He read for the role of Dr. Goebbels and didn't get the part." Having watched him work the crowd that evening, I sometimes thought he perhaps should have been given the role. When I asked Wynn about the man who defended the piece, he gave me his name (again, clearly Jewish) and said, "He was one of my students, too. He tried out for Göring; he didn't get that part, either."

This was typical of responses to the work. My staunchest defenders, like my fiercest attackers, have been Jews. Unfortunately, the defenders have wielded little power in the literary world. And, as a fellow poet, also Jewish, once told me, when you considered their history, you could scarcely expect many to be entirely reasonable on this subject.

As for the reviews, Wynn had warned me that, even if they hadn't been set against the subject matter, reviewers were antagonistic to this theater despite its introduction of many acclaimed writers and performers. The great surprise came when Clive Barnes wrote a glowing and highly intelligent review, fully grasping the work's aims. Yet, this too had its irony: until a few weeks before, he had been reviewer for *The New York Times* and so had powers of life and death over many productions. If his review had appeared there, we might still be running. Alas, he was now with *The New York Post*.

We ran to good houses for the scheduled performances, but advance sales would not warrant extending the run. This saddened us all; one of the actresses, Catherine Byers, offered $2,000 of her own money to keep the show alive. All said how much they had enjoyed having memorable lines to speak and that they had not worked with so strong a group in years. (That no review mentioned the quality of the acting confirmed my sense of hardened prejudice.) Of course, as soon as we announced the closing, calls for tickets flooded the box office.

Performances in several other cities followed, the first in Norfolk, where I was teaching. Next, a new script, prepared by its director, Gary Fisher, played at the Buffalo Entertainment Theater. On opening night, I was surprised to see a blank, open stage; in place of settings, the actors played in front of a screen showing documentary films of the war and of Hitler's rise to power. Several of the performances were excellent. The amateur projectionist, however, showed all the films upside down that night; afterward, several people congratulated me on this daring device!

I have noted that I wished the New York audience had seen our second, not our third, version. Or the version done in Ypsilanti, Michigan, the following year. This script was coauthored by the director, Annette Martin, who did a fine job not only with the actors but also with the script. She began by breaking the unity of many individual speeches, scrambling several together and passing lines back and forth between characters. She also restored the use of more than one actor for a role, so dramatizing the characters' inner conflicts.

At the center of an immense set stood a bust of Hitler, roughly twenty feet high and carved (with a chainsaw) out of Styrofoam. Over its face and shoulders different lights could play, seemingly changing its expression. Around the bust ranged a series of ramps, stairs, and platforms where the Chorus could hold processions, marches, or could mark off areas for individual scenes. The music, often skewed and atonal variations on Nazi marches or popular tunes of the period, was played offstage by the composer, Dick Segal.

This, indeed, produced a kind of spoken oratorio. We also brought back a device which had originated with Carl Weber and which we had tried out in New York but then had abandoned. Annette Martin felt that the piece needed a commentator, partly to lead the audience through the action, partly to confirm the audience in the sense that they should distance themselves from these characters. I agreed, but felt it was important that this commentator should not be able to take a morally superior tone. It had become central to my thinking that there must be no disclaimer.

We found our commentator in "Frau Wirtin," a figure from Renaissance songs and poems who, as defeat neared, had been resurrected by the Berliners to mock and scorn their leaders in rhymed verses, much like limericks and often quite obscene. Meaning to establish a low-down character for her, I gave her name not as the literal "Madame Innkeeper," but as "Old Lady Barkeep." We actually used a few of the verses Carl Weber remembered from wartime days and I wrote many more, which introduced characters, commented on the action, and sneered at the Nazis' lack of loyalty or backbone.

In this production, of course, we were dealing with an entirely different league of performers. Some of the students had had considerable college stage experience but several had never been on a stage before. Annette Martin handled this cast splendidly, marshaling them into squadron maneuvers and processions onstage, teaching them to project character, sometimes even teaching basic voice production. Still, only so much is possible. Several of the cast were very good; the one really superlative performance was given by Laila Farah Mohtar, who had recently emigrated from Beirut and who played Old Lady Barkeep. Heavy-bodied and tough-looking, her voice rang like a stevedore's; she drove the whole production.

Several years later, in 1991 or '92, I received a telephone call from Carl Weber. He was coming to Newark, Delaware, where I was teaching, for a conference on Brecht and had some interesting news. Peter Von Becker, a prominent German director who was a friend of his, had told him that in the area of (formerly East) Berlin where Hitler's bunker had been they were excavating for a complex of expensive buildings. Now, they kept discovering extensions of the bunker network that they'd not known about, were bringing out all sorts of items: mementos, old uniforms, official files. On the site of the actual bunker they planned to build a theater; Von Becker was interested in performing our stage piece there. I arranged to meet Carl for lunch the next day.

This, of course, was fiercely exciting. I had visited that spot twice since the war. Once, as part of that visit when I interviewed Speer, I had crossed the border with my wife and son at Checkpoint Charlie and, the cold war still raging, had gone into East Berlin looking for the place where the actual bunker had been. I knew that it had been burned out, then flooded, by the Russians; I'd been told that it was nothing but a field with a bump in the middle. Yet I felt that at the actual site, after so much reading, I'd discover some important idea. Down the dreary streets of East Berlin, between rows of cement-block apartment houses, empty except for security forces, I walked till I found what I took for the spot. It seemed safe to walk into the field, toward the Berlin Wall itself, because I was wearing a white raincoat and obviously not sneaking or hurrying. At once I was surrounded by jeeploads of East German soldiers. They were reasonable and polite, telling me that this wasn't even the right field—it was two blocks further on. I could walk down there, but mustn't go into the field. My friends had been right—it was a bump in a field. I went back to join my wife and son for a cup of bitter coffee in a sad little bar.

Years later, with Kathy, my present wife, I had stayed in a year-old luxury hotel perhaps two blocks from the bunker site; we were in Berlin for a conference. Checkpoint Charlie had been dismantled. A taxi took us to our meetings across the former border, though the driver had to consult his map—a year before, it had been illegal even to own a map of West Berlin. Our hotel was incredibly luxurious; our conference paid for the room, but we could only afford to eat there once. Down the center of the vast, three-storied lobby, a waterfall cascaded; beside those gushing waters, a man in a tuxedo played an ivory piano. The revolving entrance door, as large as most family dining rooms, turned automatically at your approach. In the display windows at its sides were enough cut flowers for a statesman's or a gangster's funeral.

Now it seemed I might go back a third time, for the performance of my poems about that place's history. But when I woke the day I was to meet Carl, I couldn't move my left arm. The first doctor thought I had a pinched nerve; the next—and all others since— decided this was a TIA (Transient Ischemic Attack), not exactly a stroke, but close. By the next day, my arm had recovered but Carl had left. Though I wrote both to him and to Von Becker, the project apparently fell through.

Looking back, it seems unlikely that to disable oneself at just that moment was purely coincidental. First, I wondered whether I could coalesce the several stage versions—especially when many completed poems hadn't been included and others were still to be written. It was imperative to finish the cycle of poems first. And there were moral qualms. Though much obloquy and blame had been cast against this work, I had never doubted that its aim was ethical and anti-fascistic. Yet one could not predict the result of such a production—neo-Nazis were springing up in Germany and else-where. The stage piece would surely be inimical to them, but one could never predict events or what people would understand. After all, Lorca's political leanings had been, if anything, toward the Right but he had been executed by Rightists, partly because his songs had been picked up and used by the Left. Who could guess the effect of bringing Hitler's figure so sharply into German minds at this point?

Or was I afraid of the notoriety and "success" this production might bring? Clearly, I had once been frightened and blocked by the Pulitzer Prize my first book had won. Had I escaped that fear? Though I resented the isolation and accusation this project had brought me, might that have been a blessing in disguise? At least I had been left alone, free from the pressures of American literary politics and publicity. I'd been able to pursue my work, no matter who disapproved. Surely I'd been luckier than some who wrote unpopular poems, and perhaps luckier than some others who had too eagerly sought popularity.

Of course, I hoped that the ethical considerations were pri-mary, hoped that fear or weakness hadn't prevailed. Still, if I understood Simone Weil, ethics was always the flag of the power-less. Perhaps all my self-questioning was extraneous; mightn't the added tension of anticipating this discussion have caused a momentary fault in the blood flow? By now, I don't expect ever to answer these questions, yet I can't quit asking.

In 1994 I retired from teaching at the University of Delaware; Kathy and I returned to the old house in the woods outside Erieville, New York. Although at first I had worried that she might not like such isolation, she was by now even fonder of the place than I was. I would have gladly moved to Mexico where we went to escape the winters, to Louisiana or to any warmer climate where we had friends. She had grown so attached to the house, though, and we had invested so heavily fixing it up that it seemed absurd to leave; besides, every third house in the area was already for sale. Who would buy ours? We settled down—with two households' worth of furniture—to work on those projects that, until now, we had always had an excuse for not finishing.

For me, this meant, first, completing the cycle. I had no schema for the overall shape, trusting that a form would create itself if I merely wrote poems for each character as I became interested. That had happened with *Heart's Needle*—why not now? Of course, I might have to write new pieces to create this shape, but I trusted I could let that develop naturally.

By this time, there were roughly seventy poems, which I divided into seven sections according to theme and the advancing battle for Berlin. It seemed, again, that some sort of commentary or narration was necessary though I was still determined to use no one who could take a morally superior stand. I began by introducing each section with a quotation: Thucydides, Machiavelli, Simone Weil, etc. Though this helped clarify my thinking, it seemed too somber for a work already plentifully dark. I returned to my earlier commentator, Old Lady Barkeep, dug up the verses I'd written and made more. For the cycle's first section, I gave her one poem introducing each character; after that, one poem to begin each section. This, I thought, had the quality I needed and, feeling if as someone had lifted a truck off my shoulders, I sent the manuscript to Al Poulin before we left for Mexico that November.

There, I happened to need a copy of the earlier unfinished edition and called the BOA office. They had no standard copies left—instead they loaned me one from the expensive specially bound edition. I opened it and found, to my horror, that two poems of Joseph Goebbels' had been left out of my new manuscript. This may seem absurdly inept but, by this time, there were some eighty-seven poems. Easy enough to forget whether a particular piece was present in so large a manuscript. Now, in Mexico, I had to redate several poems, reposition them in the cycle, and make whatever revisions this entailed. Again, I sat back and sighed.

Next came a call from Poulin: Irving Berlin's estate had refused rights for "Say It Isn't So," which Eva Braun sang in one of her poems. This was not, as we had feared, to hide the fact that many of the Nazis had liked his songs, but rather that, in the same poem, there were also words by other American song-writers. Berlin's songs must not appear interspersed with anyone else's lyrics. Al wanted to drop the song altogether. I was opposed: all Eva's poems used songs to reach toward her unconscious thoughts and feelings. I decided to make new words saying much the same things but still singable to that melody. The song that had been "Say It Isn't So" now reads, as translated from English into English, "Tell Me It's Not True"—not exactly a distinguished translation.

One other substitution was necessary: for the book's cover I had wanted to use the X-ray of Hitler's skull taken in September, 1944, and reproduced in Werner Maser's, *Hitler: Legend, Myth and Reality*. Unable to obtain the rights to this X-ray, BOA's managing editor obtained an anonymous skull X-ray of an apparently deceased individual, from a Rochester medical imager. However, when the imager heard the title, *The Führer Bunker*, he hedged on the deal and called a local bookstore to ask the proprietor if he'd ever heard of BOA Editions. When the proprietor assured him that BOA was a legitimate press, he released the X-ray.

After that, things went smoothly. The book appeared and, as expected, was completely ignored by the most influential publications—mostly in New York. The strongest disapproval of my work had always centered there; that has not altered, if I am to judge by the reading I gave soon thereafter at the Manhattan Theater Club—twenty people came, five of them on the theater staff. I am always astonished when I give readings elsewhere to find that through the rest of the country I am well-received and my work well-known.

Outside New York, the book received some very strong reviews; letters of approval came from readers around the country. Fit audience though few, I tried to convince myself. Four new essays about my poems and criticism appeared in the British magazine, *Agenda*. My friend, the poet Leszek Szaruga, translated Magda Goebbels' poems into Polish; another Polish friend found their accuracy and recreation of the difficult verse forms astonishing.

So I began to read these poems in public again. I had tried that some years before, but audiences went away looking as if I had spoken a foreign language. I had felt that to charge large fees (which I needed), then send people away dissatisfied, seemed improper. On the other hand, it seemed at least equally improper to read only what people wanted and already liked, especially when I strongly suspected that these were my best poems. I also thought the poems were saying something people needed to know about themselves and their world—which may suggest that I harbor some of that sense of moral superiority I am quick to condemn in others. I compromised by always including one poem from the cycle— usually Eva Braun's "Tea for Two" poem—in my other readings. In 1995, however, I was invited to give a full reading from the cycle in Claremont McKenna College's yearly Holocaust Memorial. This (though a bad head cold put me in danger of losing my voice) went very well. Next, I was invited to read at Frostburg, Maryland, for the fifty year memorial of the end of World War II and, finally, at my old campus at Newark, Delaware. Each reading had gone better than the one before and each audience seemed more appreciative.

The greatest surprise came from the least likely place. A young American, Collin McMahon, who'd been raised in Germany and still lived there, wanted to translate a selection from the cycle. I offered to help identify the poems' many quotations, little realizing that this was precisely what I could not do—since I had read only the books translated into English, I had never seen the original German statements and might not have recognized them if I had. (I have always given thanks that I could read neither French nor German; the research would have been endless.) Besides, though I had kept all the books I'd used, when I went back to them I almost immediately was sniffling and sneezing, my head and nose filling, my eyes running. Stored in our unheated house for many winters, the books had collected dampness and a rich crop of mold—my allergies to this sometimes sent me to bed for ten days at a time. I could only continue if I wore a face mask and rubber gloves; I soon had to stop even that. I felt guilty but not really sorry—I was thoroughly sick of everyone's lies and excuses about the war. I gave him little help, yet McMahon produced (so far as I could judge) excellent and lively translations. Now *he* can deal with getting them accepted, published, or performed in, of all places, Germany. I wish him all the luck in the world.

XII. YOUR OWN FOOTPRINTS

Trundling our luggage into the side entrance of that same Best Western where I'd stayed years ago when visiting my parents, we found our way blocked by just the sort of chaos I'd always found at my parents' house—here made up of tables, chairs, potted plants and bulletin boards. Here, too, seemingly from my mother's era, were six or eight white-haired ladies clambering through the squalor, checking lists, signing papers, chatting excitedly. "Is this the place?" I asked my wife, "All this confusion; these people!" "What else?" she asked, pointing to an orange-and-black banner on the wall:

> BEAVER FALLS HIGH SCHOOL
> CLASS OF 1943, 50TH REUNION

After all, I'd seen most of these people at the reunion fifteen years before; how could they have become so suddenly decrepit? How could the girls I'd known, many of them dauntingly desirable, wane into these comfy grandmothers? Surely, I wasn't of this year and model?

Checked in, we fled to our room to ask ourselves if we really wanted to face this. Courage gradually renewed by showers and fancy garb, we ventured down to the dinner-dance. At the door we were met by a friendly Black man I greeted as "Jake." He blinked, but proceeded to nametag me: DEWITT—a name I hadn't heard in years. Nowadays strangers call me "Bill"; friends call me "De." That evening, I was "DEwitt"—like that Navy dialect where misbehavior puts you on the "REpoat." Or as if my name meant "to remove intelligence." Had I been called that? Surely, transmogrifications of "Snodgrass" had been bad enough! (My younger brother had at least borne the amusing nickname: "Sneezeweed.") Still, I knew my memory was faulty; I soon learned that the man at the door had always been "James," never "Jake."

Inside, a favorite diversion was to go from table to table, covering your nametag and asking, "Guess?" An embarrassing game: if you missed, that could mean, "I didn't know you very well," or, "You've grown too old to tell." Worse, many names I had hoped to find were not there—some lived too far away, some had stopped living. Every girl I had ever pursued turned up missing. The only one I'd ever dared ask to dance had come from a nearby country community, was indeed farm-fresh and actually named Nell; she'd fallen ill and died two days before graduation. The object of my first grade crush—vaunting the related but tonier name Ellen—had married money, gone alcoholic and, they said, was too toplofty for such events. The ballet dancer I'd lacked the nerve to pursue (or even to stand still and get caught by) had married a soldier and gone to Germany. She, for whom sensuous movement was everything, had been paralyzed by multiple sclerosis, then died in her twenties. Finally, that willowy maiden—named Willa—whom I had pestered all through junior high school, whose house I had nightly dawdled past whistling sad songs, married one of the town bullies. They had moved to San Antonio where once, on a reading tour, I visited their home. Socially prominent, a Girl Scout executive, she was still limp, pretty, and distant; he owned a hardware business, was energetic, curious about my writing, fun to talk to.

One of the first women I did encounter—Ada Ann Steele, whom we had admiringly nicknamed, "Stainless"—was now Ada Ann Ohnezeit. Since she seemed as handsome, amiable, and lively as ever, I suggested we relabel her "Timeless." She looked at me askance; polylingual puns are not improved by commentary.

Gloria Boulding, tall and black, who had been one of the brightest students, seemed less tarnished by age than patined. She and I had competed for honors and for class office. She was now retiring as head nurse from the local hospital; friends said she was embittered by this humbler career. No doubt much potential had been wasted there; still, I knew patients who were grateful she'd chosen that profession. At the dance she was jauntily dressed and had maintained an imperious carriage, seemed proud of what she'd done. No handsomer grandmother exists.

Most women who'd stayed in town seemed older and less interesting, though most had done something fascinating—they had raised children. But they could say little about this beyond addresses and statistics—partly because we raise children instinctively, not really knowing what we do. Besides, we aren't allowed to discuss those problems we *do* understand. What you *could* talk about—without sounding like an afternoon TV show—were shifts in status: how some from middle-class families had failed notably; others from poorer families had made remarkable successes.

Marching with a bassoon in the school band, Olga Vekasy had seemed awkward and blockish, rough-hewn out of oak. At our reunion fifteen years before, you'd have thought she'd met a fairy godmother. An important buyer for a Cleveland department store, she was glamorously outfitted, graceful on the dance floor. Afterward, she and I had driven around, then parked on a hill overlooking the town to reminisce. I sang her several Hungarian songs I was translating. She now reported that when we'd arrived at a friend's early-morning breakfast party there had been amused whispers. Nothing whisperable had happened.

A year or two later, passing through Cleveland, I had dialed her number. A man answered: "She's not here, pal. Who's calling?" At the reunion, divorced, she was again transformed. Scouting out her background, she'd visited Budapest, then stayed to learn the language and soak up history and culture. As she aged, her angles were reasserting themselves; she again seemed not just tall but big. She wore peasant colors, a garish clash of styles; her conversation was vulgar, urgent, and enormous fun.

As my father's career had grown, we moved from house to house, each area bringing new neighbors, new schools, new classmates. The boys I'd known from prosperous families had been reasonably successful—often taking over family businesses—yet now seemed depleted and worn. The comical types I'd always been drawn to seemed overdetermined to prove they were still clever or else that they'd become wise and solid.

Like my friend Olga, some of the boys from immigrant families had found livelier successes. My mother's erstwhile cleaning woman was a Croat who had fled Yugoslavia and the Serbs. Whenever her son, John Smolich, had come to tell us she couldn't work that day, we knew that her husband, drunk again, had beaten her up. Once or twice, we'd had to go rescue her or take her for treatment. After graduation, John had moved to Philadelphia and become involved in party politics. Expensively dressed, he now walked with a swagger and glad-handed us all like potential voters. Ignored while in school, he was instantly popular.

The boys—again, like the girls—that I most wanted to see were missing. At the time John's mother worked for us, we'd lived in a middle-class enclave called Lincoln Place; my best friends had been Bus Windon, from a poorer area on one side, and Elisha Grant, a chunky, genial kid from a Black area on the other. Elisha—'Lishe—played tuba in the band, bringing it home each night to practice. Twice a day we walked to school and back, the tuba coiled around his shoulders like a chrome-plated sea beast marshalling our progress to the bass patterns of all the popular marches.

No one now knew where they were or even if either was still alive, though I later learned that both were living only a few miles away. After the war, 'Lishe had found a niche as janitor at the high school, where the band made him a sort of mascot. Then he'd been arrested, in a town downriver, as a Peeping Tom. Since his behavior may have resulted from a wartime cranial injury, he was sentenced only to a period of treatment. But the high school job was lost. He moved to a nearby town, looked after by an older, heavy Black woman. When I'd hunted him up, fifteen years before, he seemed troubled by my presence; she seemed antagonistic. It was not likely he'd attend a fancy-dress occasion partly designed for people to display successes.

On our daily marches, a fourth boy, Fred Shook, had sometimes joined us. He'd gotten in trouble once for smuggling his grandfather's brass-and-chrome pistol into summer camp. Later, he recruited several of us to lift trinkets from the local five-and-ten; I soon lost nerve, though, and convinced others to quit. He too was missing; in Florida he had signed many checks "Ben Hogan"—whom he *did* resemble—and had done serious time.

There were other absences. Before arriving, I had wondered about Al Carbone, a former football lineman who'd been voted onto a nearby town council. At the earlier reunion, he'd shouted across the room that he wanted to pull my beard "to see if it was real." On the dance floor, he did just that—not exactly blowing it in my face, but making a clear challenge. I was glad to be too old to get into a brawl, but said loudly, "Al, you got to watch that kind of stuff—I've got a Polish wife now and you might get hurt!" Would he step up the ante now that I was with a younger, Irish wife? No; cancer had taken him two years before.

Generally, age had been roughest on those we'd thought most durable, the athletes. Big Ray Bentley, a lineman who had also wrestled professionally, was hugely present though his own bout with cancer had left him a shambling wreck. Worse off was our former star halfback, Loyal Bricker. Broken field runners had carried a special glamour; besides, he'd been friendly, confident, and spectacularly handsome. On the field's edge, warming up with high knee lifts, his uniform had flexed like a stallion's flank. By now, his name had become the saddest of ironies. He had married a majorette, Barbara Goll, tall and sturdy, her flanks even more generally admired than his. Graduating from our local Covenanter college, he took over his family's nearby ice-cream store. Then a series of sexual affairs with coeds—sometimes several at once— burst into scandal; the store was closed.

Though very ill—no one specified an ailment—he had come, still with his wife, to the dance. Shrunken and drawn, he exuded defeat and apology. In a black suit, stiff white shirt, and somber necktie he looked eerily like a Colonial New England preacher. Barbara, seemingly taking on the weight and solidity he'd lost, looked like Dürer's *Fortuna*, heavy and scornful. She sat to one side, surrounded by other women, observing her husband and the general scene with distaste.

Walking now and then to the edge of the floor, Loyal took snapshots of the dancing couples; no one asked for copies or for photographs with him. He came once to our table to praise my wife's looks, then a second time to say, "You did it right, DEwitt; you did it right." If he meant my marriage, I *had* finally got that right. But that was sheerest luck —the trail of loves, marriages, and divorces that led me here had surely been as foolish and as harmful as his infidelities. If I had stumbled to a better destination, he'd probably had the jollier voyage.

The greatest success and the worst scandal in our class had

befallen Bernard Linder, whose family had once lived next door. Years later I'd run into him in Norfolk where he was an accountant; I'd hired him to handle my taxes. He had since died of a heart attack. In Youngstown, he had built a remarkable financial empire. When this collapsed—he clearly implied that his methods had been questionable—headlines had also proclaimed that he kept a "love nest" in an exclusive part of town. In this cruel way, he'd said, his wife had learned of his infidelity and came to his office carrying the paper. She had asked one thing: "What did I do wrong?" He looked at me straight and said, "That's when I learned what *I'd* done wrong!" After his death, she made a modest estimate of what I still owed him. I wanted but never found a way to tell her that this intimation of her loyalty and of his self-recognition had left me with a psychic debt not so easily paid.

At our table were two couples I had never known well. Leslie Demeter had always seemed puzzling—lively, yet never quite attached to any group and, so, nearly absent. He revealed now that in school, and on the streets, he was picking up English and hurrying home to teach it to his Hungarian mother. He and his wife—also a classmate—did not seem openly antagonistic to each other, but there was obviously little communication. Retired, he spent much of his time in his basement ham radio shack, talking long-distance to friends he had never seen.

Joseph Wachter, also at our table, had always seemed—not exactly aggressive, but surly, full of pent-up angers. These had found their object: the Japanese. He described, proudly, his trips to Pearl Harbor to view the sunken ships, visit museums, read official reports. Perhaps friends or relatives had been killed there; perhaps his German surname still provoked a need to preserve anti-Axis feelings. Perhaps one's hatreds simply needed a target.

And there *were* economic reasons. He and Demeter, like their immigrant fathers, had worked in the local mills and foundries. You could argue, without too much exaggeration, that we had fought two world wars to protect those mills—with the industries they headed and symbolized—against German and Japanese competition. If the Germans produced better steel, better tools, better machinery, while the Japanese made these things cheaper, how else could you keep them out of the market? During the war, while bombing those industries, we talked about making Germany once more an agricultural nation and of handing over its patents, as had been done after World War I, to the French. Similar suppressions were planned against Japan. The men sitting here were among those who'd fought and believed they had won that second, most terrible, war. It certainly appeared now that if we, as a country, had not lost the peace, we as workers had. American money was finding it cheaper to buy into the enterprises it had planned to quash. Rebuilt and up-to-date, basic industries in Germany and Japan were flourishing; ours were being sold off, shut down, or moved to places where workers were weaker and poorer, where government regulation had been less restrictive.

Some months earlier, planning for this visit, I had phoned the local Board of Trade to ask if one could visit the Babcock and Wilcox Tube Company, where I had worked briefly in my teens. Small compared to such behemoths as Bethlehem Steel or Jones & Laughlin, it was still the largest plant in our area, one on which the city chiefly depended. The Board knew only that the plant was closed. Then a secretary recalled vaguely that another company was renting space there and continuing a small operation. Following this lead, I learned that B & W had fallen to one of the earliest hostile takeovers; sections of the company had been sold, the remainder bought by PMAC: Property Management Acquisitions Corporation. Eventually, I contacted Paul Carver, a former B & W man who'd been brought back to manage the sale of used machinery and to rent space in vacant buildings. He arranged for me to accompany him on his rounds the day following our reunion.

Earlier that day, my wife and I had driven around to see how the town had fared. Residential areas seemed much as I remembered; downtown, nothing was the same. My grandfather's house with his office jutting out above the main street was now gone, a gap like an extracted tooth; behind, the firehouse and jail appeared. Many storefront windows were smeared over or boarded up; the surviving businesses seemed afterthoughts, makeshifts. The big hotel had, for a while, housed the elderly; now, like all three movie houses, it was closed. No one under middle age appeared on the streets. The local foundries and smaller industries—Armstrong Cork, Mayer China, Ing-Rich Enameling, Moultrop and Crucible Steel—were either closed or dormant.

Wanting to scout the layout of the B & W plant before my scheduled visit there, we tried to drive around that property. As the operation had grown, it had spread out over the hillier, wooded regions at the upper end of town, then expanded into several smaller locations farther off. Still covering a large area there, it was surrounded by the frame houses of those families whose menfolk had worked there. The main plant seemed completely abandoned, the gates and high fences locked, the long corrugated iron sheds behind them rusting or broken through, partially painted over at different times with varying colors, the windows gone or plugged up; railyards filled with rusting machinery, broken crates, half-dumped bags of concrete, other materials I could not identify. Neither could I tell, among the sheds and bays, the sub-buildings and attachments where I'd worked.

The office of PMAC, the present operators, was located on one of the main highways through the town. But one had to enter this building at the rear—as I did the following day, climbing to the second floor and a small suite of offices, tidy but simple. Carver, friendly and businesslike, offered me a cup of coffee. Soon we were joined by Ralph Morton, a former PR man with B & W; then, climbing into Carver's truck and and taking a small private road, we headed to the mill buildings. The first two long sheds had obviously been built long after I'd left the area, when the workforce had grown to over 6,000. Carver suggested that the third shed— older and blackened—was probably where I had worked. All three buildings, unlighted, seemed empty of machinery or equipment; Carver made no move toward opening them. Burning lights and the sounds of work, however, came from inside a fourth shed. When a foreman asked about me, Carver answered that I had worked here during the war and was looking for my footprints.

During the war, our section of the mill had cut small-gauged, thick-walled steel tubing into foot-long segments which would become the hinging joints for tank treads. There, as through fifteen or twenty other buildings, swarms of men, women, and boys had hustled here and there, overseen by foremen on the floor and those crane operators who rode high over each bay slinging loads of uncut tubes, raw ingots, lumber, equipment, and other materiel to new locations. The din and clangor of this work—as, no doubt, of any steelworking plant—was shattering. Soon, my ears were ringing not just when I left the plant but when I went back for the next shift, giving me good reason—or excuse?—to quit and get back to studying music.

Inside the present building were perhaps a dozen men working at "extrusion"—forcing hot metal through a shaped die's opening, thus forming wires, bars or beams. In contrast to our old coal-burning furnaces which could weigh a hundred tons, they had a small, neat, electric one—used only at night when electricity was cheaper. Much of the building stayed dark. In a second bay, nearby, a similar group worked at a "cold draw" process, finishing unheated steel. Here, also, a smaller crew still made thin tubes by "piercing"—driving metal against a pointed, stationary mandrel. In contrast to the unskilled thousands of my time, these crews—perhaps totaling thirty men—were clearly experienced and knowledgeable. Down the length of these bays the great cranes still wheeled on the building's main beams, the cab box rolling back and forth athwart the building's width. But the box was empty— the operator, once a sort of familiar deus ex machina, had been replaced by an unseen remote control.

What I had once felt were "dark, Satanic mills" belonged to another age. Our area's huge Bessemer converters, open hearths and blast furnaces that had thrown a ghastly glare over whole hillsides of frame houses, stores, rocky cliffs and woods, the eerie slag that poured out like molten lava along the riverbanks in towns like Ambridge, Midland, and Aliquippa would never exist again— not, at any rate, in *this* country. The rolling mills, rough finishing, steel melting and various hot-plants, the stock sheds and machine shops, pickling, scarfing and hammering operations—all were gone, their equipment sold and shipped away. One of the first things Morton had said to me was, "We didn't know how good we had it." I never imagined I could feel a nostalgia for those infernal presences.

As we drove through the abandoned grounds, I *could* identify the office buildings —made of the same orange brick as my parents' home —where I'd once punched in for work and collected my pay. These were well past repair; ceilings had fallen in, walls collapsed; all were boarded over, chained shut, plastered with NO TRESPASSING signs.

Later that day we took Carver's advice and drove to Aliquippa, the site of Jones & Laughlin, once the world's largest steel mill. And where I, in the months before I got drafted, had spent night after night courting the girl, Lila, who after the war became my first wife. Along the river, where the seemingly innumerable mill buildings had been, stood a single long mill shed, possibly still in use. The intricate webwork of interconnecting railway tracks had narrowed to a single line. From a distance, the riverside area looked as if it had been emptied, raked, then sprinkled with clean white sand—a little like a Japanese temple garden. "Round the decay of that colossal wreck . . . ," I chanted to myself. A friend involved in reclamation said it was costing more to clear up these mills' pollution than it would have cost to bring them up to operating standards.

Up from the river, in the cramped area of downtown Aliquippa, we saw what my own city could well become. Once crowded and violent, nearly half its buildings had been torn down; those left had broken or patched windows, nailed or padlocked doors. The lots between were strewn with old stone and brickwork, weeds, rubble, garbage. Two storefronts not boarded up housed revivalist churches. The sides of buildings still standing were covered with spray-painted graffiti or with large murals (several, surprisingly well done) of religious scenes and calls to redemption.

There, among the ruined two- and three-story brick buildings and empty trash-filled lots, stood—like a concrete pillbox in a field of ruins—a one-story tile-coated White Tower Hamburger joint. Fifty years before, I had come down here every night from the pleasant middle-class suburb where my girl lived. My head spinning with romantic ideals and my groin racked by retracting unspent sperm—a familiar pain we knew as "parlor balls"—I had sat on one of the little stools there among gamblers, mafiosi, prostitutes, and J & L workers. Sometimes I ordered a flat, greasy hamburger to convince the waitress I had some right to loiter there till my bus would take me back to Beaver Falls.

After the war, that young woman married me, bore a child, divorced me, remarried, then was widowed; she had been a grade-school teacher, a hospital clerk, an EEG technologist, a coin machine attendant, and is now a retiree living in Florida. I married three other women, worked in a hotel, a hospital, and a college library, taught at half a dozen universities, had been alternately honored and berated as a writer, and now lived half the year in upstate New York, half in Mexico. Some things abide: the White Tower would offer its clientele, now mostly Black, the same flat and greasy hamburgers.

One change seemed an undeniable improvement: that orange brick house where I'd passed my teens. Within some twenty years, my mother had managed to convert this handsome building into a gigantic trash bin. After her death, my sister Shirley and her family had spent months hauling out rubbish, then vacuuming, scouring, waxing, airing-out and de-scenting. Still, the house went unsold; during the general economic collapse of the '80s, many fine houses, offered for a pittance, still stood vacant. So my sister had put this house into the keeping of her daughter Barbara—named for my sister who had died in the house years before. This second Barbara must have been more headstrong and less easily managed than her aunt: she had not only spotted signs of decay and protected the house from vandals; she had changed it.

The day after my mill tour, we visited this house which had evoked such violent emotions from me. We had actually been told Barbara had "transformed" it but that was too extreme, even somehow reductive. It was more as if she had mollified it, brought it around to be reasonable, to relax. Once relaxed, its jumble of discordances and stifling passions dispersed; light, air, and calm could be reinstalled.

What we first noticed, as we had at the party or the mills, were things missing, all that we didn't see. Here, though, absences were blessings. In the glassed-in porch and the foyer around the central stairs, there were no boxes of broken toys and children's games, wrecked wagons or tricycles, folded-down card tables, foldup coffee stands, coat racks with snarled wire hangers. Between ourselves and the living room no strings of jangling bells, gongs, finger cymbals hung, waiting to entangle you—a single string remained, off to one side. That room now held only one couch, one piano, one television, two stuffed chairs. Around the fireplace, the thick, black paint had been stripped, leaving a pleasant area of tilework. The built-in glass-fronted bookcases had been cleared of their chaos of books, figurines, snapshots, tea sets. Two of the cheap tapestries—clashing with the room and with each other—had vanished.

In the dining room, the banquet table had given place to one of mere family size. Modest wallpaper replaced yet another tapestry. The second television set, the sewing machine, the huge buffet—its top buried under gray rumpled doilies and napkins, brass stands with obeisant candles, fruit bowls and saucers piled with buttons, coins, paper clips, bubblegum, erasers—all had erased themselves. In the kitchen, the extra stove and oven, the mangle, the radio and third television, the fuzz-coated pots and pans on the walls, the dog and cat bowls, the tattered newspapers around the floor—had sublimed away. Just disposing of excess furnishings, paraphernalia and trinkets must have supplied secondhand shops for twenty miles around.

On the second floor we found one pleasing addition, or rather, restoration. The immense stained glass window was shining again at the head of the stairs—Barbara had bought it back from my brother and reinstalled it. Now the murky hallways on each side of the stairwell had been emptied of waist-high piles of books; the walls, once the color of dried blood, were light and creamy. Along one side, both bedrooms had been cleared and tidied as if for guests; Barbara herself slept in the vast master bedroom on the other side where once my mother had threaded paths through stacks of clutter. Both bathrooms had been stripped of their black paint, the woodwork restored to a clear oak finish.

The third floor was surely where I'd find the most and the darkest footprints—much early sexual or affectional experience had centered here. When we first moved in, I had had this whole area for my own. It seemed as if, crossing from end to end, you'd need a weather report and passport. The area was still immense when cut in two so that my sister Barbara, too, could have a bedroom. In my own room I had drawn and hidden pictures of naked women; once or twice, I had leaned far out of my window to watch my sister undress next door. I had lived here briefly with my first wife; then for an interminable summer with my second wife. In time, my brother moved into what had been my room; it was from there he had run across to her room when Barbara had died.

Then, after years of using my allergies to avoid staying in either room, I did come to sleep there once again. I had been living near Syracuse, New York, where I was teaching; my brother lived in San Francisco where he was a construction inspector and, on the side, wrote poems, stories, and made beautiful platinum prints of his own photographs. During the mid-70s, however, a group of these prints had been rejected for a major show; almost simultaneously, his long-term marriage had dissolved. He resigned his job, sold his cameras and moved to the Syracuse area. When he left there, about a year later, my wife also moved out. She had been profoundly important to me; he was the only member of my family to whom, for very long, I had felt close.

For a while, this matter was disguised. Then, some months after our divorce, I spent a period of residence at the Virginia Center for the Creative Arts. There a young woman introduced herself to me, saying, "I knew who you were before you even came in the room. Your laugh is exactly like your brother's—he's at the arts colony in Taos where I just came from." I saw my chance to resolve all riddles with a small ploy: "That redheaded woman he was living with—are they still together?" "I don't know," she hesitated. "I didn't get along much with him. I thought she was sterling, though. I guess they're having a rough time."

They had separated soon after that and he had gone back to Beaver Falls, moving in with our mother and taking Barbara's room. At that point my mother's faculties were so weakened with age that he and she had little contact—he would let her know whether he was in or out by placing a scarf on one of her pot-metal swordsmen downstairs. Reputedly, he was also able to slip a girlfriend, now and then, up to his room unnoticed.

In time, my second sister, Shirley, asked me to come for my mother's eightieth birthday celebration. I insisted that my brother and I must never be there together, so she obtained his word to stay away for several days. Wishing to see my mother, probably for the last time, I drove down—though I had borrowed from an unsuspecting friend a ceremonial kris in case my brother broke that promise. My visit, however, provoked no special altercations except for my mother's agitated scoldings at my daring to believe there could have been anything improper between my wife and brother. I said nothing although Dick had, meantime, revealed the whole affair to my daughter, Cynthia. Upstairs, I slept in Barbara's bed beside thick typescripts of unfinished novels with which he must have intended to eclipse my work. Placed conspicuously on the desk lay his letters from Camille—presumably love letters that I was meant to notice and to read. I elected to deny myself that entertainment.

For some time after my mother's death, this floor would become uninhabitable. The roof had decayed and the ceilings, like those in the tube mill's offices, had buckled. My niece Barbara, with help from her parents and a boyfriend, had had the roof repaired and was now replacing and painting those ceilings. All of this, of course, must have been expensive and many of Barbara's projects must have seemed downright heretical—Grandma Helen wouldn't have approved! Still, Barbara's family had provided funds and practical help. Flexible emotions also seemed to have been restored to the house. Barbara's family now seemed actively proud of the changes.

I would not claim that none of the useless objects, none of the old sentiments and sentimentalities remained; I have already noted the finger cymbals in the first-floor doorway. Like my mother, Barbara was a collector; like her namesake, she had a glass menagerie of china dogs, though hers were arranged in almost military order. On the third floor stood a mangle (Barbara did not know either its name or its use) and, next to it, the clumsy antique sunlamp we had always tried to get ourselves to use. Nearby, however, under ranked fluorescent lights, stood a tubular chrome frame holding trays of the seedlings (already poking up their small green tips) she was raising and would later replant in beds around the yard.

On our last evening there, my wife Kathy and I went to dinner with Barbara, her sister Hope, and their parents. A very pleasant occasion, though I could not help recalling those visits my gay great-uncle Bryce, a singer and pianist, had occasionally paid my family fifty years before. Like my father, Shirley's husband Rusty was a CPA and now ran the company my father had wanted me to inherit. Like my sisters, both my nieces worked for their father; they were becoming CPAs, so making good my apostasy. I probably seemed as foreign as we once thought Bryce, who sang Moussorgsky's "Sunless Cycle" and taught us how to say "Dah-BOO-sie." I, too, had hurled myself into the arts; my sex life, too, must have seemed less than decorous—this was, after all, my 4th wife. Still, I did not read my poems or offer instruction in pronunciation.

In the course of the day, though, we were surprised by an unexpected consonance in tastes. Where one tapestry had once hung in Barbara's living room, there was now a fine reproduction of one of Monet's great water lily paintings. She seemed to know that I had long studied and then written a poem about this canvas. And she related how, on a group tour of Paris, she had dropped out from the arranged journey to Versailles, travelling alone instead, to see the encompassing and enclosing water lily series then housed in the Orangery. She spoke of this with something like veneration.

Months later, when we'd gone to Mexico for the winter, we received a note from Barbara. Her personal envelope was embossed with a cluster of cutely clothed puppies such as her mother and grandmother would have adored. The card inside, however, reproduced the same great water lily painting, its wealth of waters spreading outward toward the viewer: calm, deeply reflective, and resolved. We couldn't have been more gratified.

XIII. GIVING UP MUSIC

*What you freely relinquish can never be
taken away from you.*

That goes for music. I am forever grateful to have given it up
early. As a student, I had been a horrid violinist and bad pianist, a
fair tympanist, an enthusiastic choral conductor. But I wanted to be
an orchestral conductor and there is a disheartening condition to
that profession: they have to know *everything.* So I gave it up—and,
oddly enough, reached the same result others have found by taking
it up. Peter Everwine neglected his poetry for several years while he
learned the banjo, an instrument and skill which I mightily envy. I
asked if he mightn't take over the university's folk music course.
"Not on your life," he answered. "Music's so great a vice, I wouldn't
turn it into a virtue for anything."

Once I gave it up, music became a vice for me too, and assumed
a pervasive influence no virtue has ever assumed. Such renuncia-
tions, of course, have great secondary advantages. Take, for in-
stance, my mournful tale of how two years in the Navy and the wish
to marry had cost me a career in music! Imagine the sympathy this
lament evoked in young women—even in my wife! I no doubt
modeled my story on the Duke of Windsor's who, we believed,
gave up an empire for the woman he loved. For the truly spiritual,
I implied, music's empire was scarcely inferior.

If there were other rewards—or other causes—the Duke and I
said little about those. After all, I was leaving a field where I was
poorly equipped—surely in training and self-discipline, perhaps in
talent. I was evading an inevitable confrontation where flair, enthu-
siasm, and fakery would not have saved me. Better, music soon took
on the glamour of the forbidden. How quickly vanished that sense
of drudgery and halfheartedness while practicing (or staring at a
music score and *not* practicing)—feelings attendant upon virtues.
No longer a duty, music became a way to evade other duties; once
forsworn, music proved a constant and satisfying mistress.

Nonetheless, I did have a wife and, before long, a child; I needed some way to support them—or a plausible excuse for failing to do so. As I've related earlier, I drifted out of music, into theater, then into the Poetry Workshops of the State University of Iowa. In time, I learned the kind of poem taught there—quirky, though certainly better than what *I'd* have devised on my own. Our models were the English Metaphysicals and the French Symbolists—the most conscious and intellectual of poets yoked together with the most unconscious and deranged. The one thing they shared was obscurity. Our more recent models were likely to be Hart Crane, Dylan Thomas, and the early Robert Lowell (the only one yet in evidence). I began to find I could produce the required qualities: intellectual compression, a brilliant texture, a surcharged rhythm and rhetoric.

Then one day, scrubbing the floor of the little Quonset hut where we lived, I heard a voice; I halted like Saul on the road to Damascus and was changed. The voice—my *tenor ex machina*—was that of the great Swiss singer, Hugues Cuénod. The campus radio station was playing his album` *Spanish and Italian Songs of the 16th and 17th Centuries,* which, after forty-five years and a thousand other tenors, still sends shivers down my back. It had everything my poems lacked: emotional intensity, passion and a clear delineation of that passion's impulse and development.

True, this first jolt needed reinforcement: that came from Randall Jarrell, who helped turn me from the high-flown intellection and ornamental rhetoric I'd so diligently learned; it came from a psychotherapy that consisted, really, of stating the problem over and over until I dropped the learned terminology and got it down into my own voice; from the young Irish student-poet John Montague, who complained that American poems hadn't any *place*, happened in never-never land; from my fellow student, Robert Shelley, who suddenly stopped imitating Hart Crane and wrote, before his suicide, half a dozen exquisite lyrics in a simple and pellucid style we'd been told was impossible in our complex world; finally, from my entanglement with two other groups of songs. But I think Cuénod's stridently passionate Renaissance songs stirred me first and most deeply.

The other songs were by Mozart and Mahler. When my first marriage broke apart, I moved into a dank cellar, where, strangely, the last tenant had left a recording of *The Magic Flute*. I had never heard it—can that be true?—and fell hopelessly in love with Papageno's arias. Soon, I was trying to translate them to sing in English. When, like everyone else, I failed at this, I turned to make my own poem on the subject, "Papageno," addressed to the girl who later became my second wife.

What attracts like the impossible? I also tried to translate Mahler's *Kindertotenlieder (Songs for the Death of Children)*—settings of poems by Rückert. Not knowing German—I always claim, half joking, it's easier to translate that way—I turned for help to my teacher, Paul Engle, who acutely singled out the turns and twists of language that made them so poignant. All the same, recognizing those effects and recreating them in another language proved to be two very different things.

I gave up on the Mahler songs and the Mozart arias but never stopped trying, even after these songs had helped lead me into my own voice and subjects, to translate Cuénod's Renaissance songs. To my surprise, I found that, given time enough, I *could* make singable English versions of some of these. I decided to stop translating anything but songs. After all, other American poets were doing fine translations of poems from many languages. Here, my musical background might give me an advantage. Besides, little by little, I was slipping under the spell of the early music that rampant musicology was making, after centuries of silence, once more available.

So, after ten or fifteen years of truce, music began again to infiltrate my outskirts. You begin by singing a song or two, then you start wanting to accompany yourself. First I bought a guitar, then a *cister*—a Swedish folk lute with twelve strings—then a Renaissance lute of eleven strings, and an archlute with twenty-four. After that, a harpsichord, a virginals, and, after selling the earlier lutes, a Baroque lute of twenty-one strings. And, as I began to branch into folk ballads and folk songs, an Arabic harp or *kanun* (the psaltery King David plays in medieval manuscripts or Arabs play in bellydance joints), a Hungarian dulcimer, a Romanian *tsambal* or small cembalon (like an American hammered dulcimer), all kinds of percussion instruments.

Soon it was singing lessons and summer collegia in early music. Here, my fellow students were mostly about twenty years old—the age I'd been when I gave up music. They could do three times what I'd done at their age: all played five or six instruments, read three clefs, transposed at sight, sang like angels. If heaven isn't like working with them, I wouldn't want to go there. Every day they studied masterpieces only known to specialists when I was twenty. If I'd realized then the riches I was giving up, I might not have let it go—and probably would have lost it altogether!

In time, there were concerts with early music groups who performed my translations while I introduced the programs. Sometimes they even let me sing with the ensemble or play a tambourine. Who needs heaven?

Midway through my career, you'd never guess I'd given it up. Half my time went into practicing, copying music, trying to transcribe old notations. Half my income (after taxes [*after alimony*]) went there: records, instruments, lessons. Oskar Kokoschka said that if you live long enough, you will see your career die and be born again three times, but, just the same, the young girls are always there. He was a pessimist. *I* find there are always old songs to take to bed. If you tire of Spanish and Italian Renaissance songs, there's the French or German Renaissance. Or the Italian *lauda*, Spanish *cantigas*, German minnesingers, French trouvères, Provençal troubadours. Earlier, the *Carmina Burana*. There is so much music—and musicologists keep finding, or making, more. I have to wonder what researcher in some European library may be uncovering, even today, my true Abishag!

This long, illicit relationship with music has, of course, affected my poems. I would have thought that work with songs, which are so strictly metrical, might bring greater regularity into my own poems. Just the opposite. Though the early poems I published were often metrical, I always wrote a fair amount of free verse as well. At first, though, I published little of this, feeling I could do as well or better in tighter forms. After all, by that time free verse was, in itself, scarcely new or exciting; if I were going to take liberties, I wanted them to produce something startling. After knowing Whitman's "Out of the Cradle Endlessly Rocking," I didn't want to publish the kind of overconscious, soporific sludge I saw in the magazines.

As patterns do, this one reversed: I still wrote both free and metrical poems but felt that the metrical verse did little I hadn't already seen, so I less often published *it*. Proportionally, my free verse seemed to become stronger. This was encouraged, I thought, by two seemingly opposed factors. First, I seemed—partly just by aging, partly through a later, extensive, psychoanalysis, able to use more freedom, turning it to my own uses. Second, and paradoxically, I had discarded some freedoms which were no use to me. Translating songs helped; being so difficult, it satisfied any needs I still had for limits or hobbles.

If I'm asked why I translate songs, I try to avoid the good commonsense answer: I want to sing the songs but can't (or don't) learn the original language. I usually try the mock-heroic: because it can't be done. This has its truth—you must not only reproduce the original's dictionary sense, but also create a satisfactory richness in your own language—give linguistic harmony and orchestration to the basic tune of literal sense. You must usually keep the original's rhyme pattern, the number of syllables, the number and position of stresses. Stress is specially troublesome: it is so distinctive in English that few singers can cope with conflicts between accent in the music and stress in the words. Further, the addition of melody to a text is almost bound to change the emotional reverberance of that text (if not, why add it?). Then, if you keep that melody but substitute a text in a new language, the new amalgam will surely have new qualities as well. This is merely to admit that you can't very often say the same thing very deeply in a second language. Even so, the local rise and fall of emotional intensity in your new text will probably have to correspond to the rise and fall in the melody and the original words. Otherwise you'll be singing some dull, function word to a high, climactic note, or you'll reach that ominous flat in the melody only to find the words saying something cheerful or flip.

Beyond all that, the song has to sing. You probably need long, open vowels for longer notes and slower passages, need to avoid consonant clusters in faster passages. This doesn't begin, however, to tell what makes one phrase sing while another won't. I've found only two books—one by W. H. Auden, one by Bainbridge Crist—which offer any real help. Mostly, you'll simply have to sing the song, the passage, the line, over and over until you find something that works. Or until you give up. That may be all right, too; if it doesn't take ten years, it may not be worth starting.

All these restrictions when translating songs tend to release me, I find, for a looser approach to my own poems. And the time spent with music gave me more confidence that I can create a satisfying music for a poem without a formal metrical system. For me: no music, no poem. Yet most of us are deficient in these areas; our sense of rhythm has been so simplified by nineteenth-century classical music and, worse, twentieth-century dance music—by that insistent thump, thump, thump; that settled 2/4, 3/4, 4/4, 6/8—that few of us produce interesting rhythms. Our metrical systems, per contra, do offer built-in tensions more striking than what many of us invent by ourselves. Still, I wanted complex, exciting rhythms outside the metrical systems; I doubt that I'd have dared try if I weren't daily saturated in music.

The vibrance (hence the tone quality) of any musical instrument with a wooden sounding board—a lute, guitar, violin, even a piano—must be developed by playing it, by its own vibrations. Someone theorized that the Stradivarius violins were so splendid because they'd been built with wood from torn-down cathedrals, wood that had been resounding for years with the choirs singing there, so developing a great vibrancy and resonance. I don't suppose that's true; an artist could choose a worse myth.

My first attempts here followed Whitman's technique of stating a pattern of sounds, then working variations on it. As I've described this elsewhere in some detail, I'll only specify the theme rhythms I took. For "Owls," I took the great horned owl's call, HOO hoo HOO, HOO, HOO; for "Old Apple Trees," I took an old show tune: "We're having a heat wave, a tropical heat wave." In a poem on Van Gogh's "Starry Night," every line (except for quotations) is based not on a rhythm but on the vowel patterns of Van Gogh's last words, "*Zóó heen kan gaan.*"

As time passed, however, I have tended to build less from variations—from basically similar motions—using, instead, direct oppositions. This has come as much from musical as from literary examples. True, one does find similar principles in literary sources—for instance, in the folk ballad (as Chesterton notes) the verses usually relate an individual's story while the chorus or refrain opposes this, both in tone and melody, with the community's response; for that matter, the folk ballad is as much a musical form as a poetic one.

Generally, the interrelations between poetry, music, and the "music of verse" are dauntingly complex and intangible. When the more accessible literal sense of the poem beckons, critics usually opt for that. Unfortunately, this leaves the impression that the poem resides in its dictionary sense, even though the least experience with translations should have dispelled such notions long ago. Since literary critics have been of little help here, I have often turned to music criticism. If I take incongruity and juxtaposition as a compositional principle, that has been shaped by studies in the classical sonata form, with its opposed themes, their development and resolution; in the Bach Fugues; or in the choruses of the *St. Matthew Passion*, with their incredible architectonics of opposed voices—voices which question, answer, lament, console, yet are perceived as simultaneously joined in a coherent structure. Music critics have long seen it as their business to analyze the emotional components of these structures, making them more available to listeners like myself.

My first attempt at this sort of construction—a poem called "After Experience Taught Me"—pitted the voice of Baruch Spinoza against that of a hand-to-hand combat instructor. In the poem "Van Gogh: The Starry Night," the main sections try to reconstruct Vincent's thoughts as revealed by the painting, but these are often interrupted by quotations from his letters or by others' letters about him. In the poem about Manet's "Execution of the Emperor Maximilian," the body of the poem consists of the thoughts of someone trying to grasp the painting, but these thoughts are interrupted by comments from historians or political writers about the historical Maximilian. The poem "A Visitation" consists of a confrontation between the speaker and his reflection, which seems to resemble Adolf Eichmann, in his large apartment window.

This was one part of a movement toward *The Führer Bunker*. I have long thought that one of the most important developments in our poetry has been the polyvoiced poem— "The Wasteland," "Naming of Parts," "The Age of Anxiety," or Henri Coulette's "The War of the Secret Agents." As I worked on these materials, it seemed that they worked best as a cycle of monologues and that the whole became a sort of oratorio for speakers.

To differentiate the voices of those in Hitler's entourage, I chose characterizing verse forms. For some, conventional forms seemed right—e.g., Magda Goebbels' villanelles, rondels, triolets. Elsewhere, free verse seemed appropriate, though this may be shaped by external elements such as Bormann's love letters, Speer's literary recollections, or musical quotations. For both Eva Braun and Hitler, music is an important feature: for her, popular songs and liturgical music; for him, the Wagnerian operas which suggest both his cravings for power and his sense of betrayal when thwarted. Dr. Goebbels' poems are interspersed with both the headlines his agencies produced and with the songs and verses he'd been reading to his children. Coming from Goebbels' almost sulfurous mouth, these produce an eerie effect: it is dismaying to be reminded that those who've committed heinous crimes for political or nationalistic ends may well be benevolent neighbors or friends, good husbands or wives, loving parents.

The arbitrary nonce forms—Speer's stepped pyramids or Himmler's graphed acrostics—are, unlike traditional verse forms, in no way involved with the creation of rhythm or music. These characters seemed to me lacking in either mental or emotional resonance. Obsession with some one quality—Himmler with order, Speer with size—has stunted or cut off other qualities, the vibrances of living beings.

Moving toward the end of this long project, I also found myself involved in other, shorter cycles of poems. It's rumored that when Tennyson could no longer stand the glossy pieties of the *Idylls of the King*, he wrote dirty limericks. When I could no longer stand the horrors of the Third Reich—and the continuing shock of finding them not so unlike other governments, other people, I have known— I turned at first to the troubadours. Later, I turned to the paintings

of the contemporary artist DeLoss McGraw. Eventually, we pro-
duced two collaborations, *The Death of Cock Robin*, then *W. D.'s
Midnight Carnival*, both books including not only the poems but
prints of the related paintings by McGraw.

In these cycles, a larger percentage of the poems is in conventional
meters. Earlier, I had done a cycle of poems about works by five post-
Impressionist painters: Matisse, Monet, Vuillard, Manet, and Van
Gogh. These poems had been in free verse, though one had a few
rhymes to make its ending more final. McGraw's paintings, mostly
watercolors and gouache, obviously demanded different treatment.
McGraw's work was superficially like a child's preschool paintings,
deliciously playful and exuberant, completely eschewing verisimili-
tude or classical perspective. I tried to match this with a sort of comic
verse (though I hoped that the darkness of the subject matter would
balance this), something almost like nursery rhymes or children's
poems.

Even here, there are likely to be as many musical quotations as
literary ones— a single poem, for instance, has quotations from:
"Buddy Boulden," "Mama Don't 'llow No Guitar Pickin'," "My
Love Is Like the Sunshine" and "Greensleeves." A *Dance Cycle*
(which McGraw has chosen not to complete) includes poems sing-
able to the melodies of Beethoven's "Minuet in G" (disguised as
F##), "Whispering," "Tales from the Vienna Woods," the "Mexican
Hat Dance," various 1930s love songs, a sixteenth century
masquerada for lute, "La *Cumparsita*," the common "apache" dance,
"Fit As a Fiddle," "The Leaves So Green," and, again, "Greensleeves."

More recently, two cycles have been inspired not by paintings
but rather specific musical performances. After hearing the pianist
Walter Ponce perform a set of Beethoven's theme and variations, I
decided to try a similar approach to the theme of autumn, each poem
broaching a different aspect of that season and using a different
metric system or a different kind of free verse. Having finished this,
I went on to try a cycle for each of the other seasons. I had earlier
published a small, beautifully printed volume with translations of
the four sonatas which accompany Vivaldi's famous concerti, *The
Four Seasons*. Since I couldn't use that title again, I called this work,
and the book where it appeared, *Each in His Season*.

Some time after I'd finished these pieces, I had the good luck to hear Garrick Ohlsson's magical recording of Chopin's Nocturnes, which led to another small cycle of five "Nocturnes." This brought me back almost uncannily to my own musical beginnings: the first recording I ever owned was of Chopin's Waltzes; after years of ignoring (and perhaps scorning) Chopin, I find it specially fulfilling to have come back to him.

Beyond these specific examples, however, I suspect that my pursuit of music has had a deep and long-abiding influence on my work in an area I've barely touched on so far. That has to do with poetry as an aural, not as a visual or intellectual, art. This appears most obviously, perhaps, in my readings of poems—my own or others'. My hosts or listeners often seem surprised that I take the matter of performance seriously—that I have selected poems to shape a program climactically, that I devote a period before a reading to breathing and vocal exercises and to concentration on these particular poems. My earliest readings—after I first received a major award—were very poor indeed. The need to reach the back rows brought on a strangled, shrieky sound. Feeling that everything in a poem was important, I tried to stress every word, almost every syllable. Worse, I tended to iron the same musical phrasing into every line. This was not much short of disastrous. If one gave only an occasional reading, I suppose one could get away with it— that might have a certain innocent and amateurish air. But I was giving many readings—and each of those ironed in the bad habits even deeper. I started taking voice lessons, first with an excellent speech teacher in Detroit, then with a series of fine singing coaches.

Clearly, this has affected the way I write. Influenced partly by the Beat poets, who gave so many readings, and by Dylan Thomas, I do compose for the voice—particularly my own voice. I feel, here, the example of the great Romantic composers—Beethoven, Brahms, Chopin, Schumann—who wrote pieces specifically for their own performances.

But that leaves me another problem also remindful of childhood faults. When I was a boy, if I was not as good as my friends at some activity, I would get my parents to buy me the expensive equipment I've already listed. Eventually, all these items collected in corners, gathering dust. Now, feeling I have little time for anything but writing, I am left with a house full of gardening tools, woodworking equipment, seasoned lumber, recording gear and all manner of musical instruments—three lutes, two guitars, several folk instruments, the *kanun*, various drums, a clavichord and a small, beautiful spinet made by Arnold Dolmetsch. I *have* sold an archlute, a lute, and a guitar, and given away the kettledrums which had lain in our garage loft since I first came to Syracuse. But we live out in the woods where there seems to be no chance—and I have little time—to advertise the other instruments. We did manage to sell our big outdated harpsichord, but only to buy a Kurzweil electronic instrument which has not only two harpsichord voices but two piano and two organ voices and, which, above all, never needs tuning. I sold one classical guitar, but soon afterward got Lucio Nuñez, a dear friend in Mexico, to make a German guitar-lute of seven strings. Giving up music may be like tobacco—it's easy; I've done it again and again.

Yet all this has a positive side. When my third wife left in 1977, I felt that I had to keep our house, though I shortly left to teach in Norfolk, Virginia, and could come back only for summers. I also bought back from my ex-wife the harpsichord I had originally bought *for* her and which we've now sold. For good. To have rebought it at that time may seem absurd—I no longer played keyboard instruments, but it had come to mean something I couldn't give up at that time. My daughter, with whom I stored the harpsichord for some years, remarked that it might seem eccentric to place an ad saying WANTED: WIFE WHO PLAYS HARPSICHORD.

Still, that is what I got in my fourth wife, Kathy. On our first date, we scarcely shook hands; on the second, I wooed her with Vivaldi and she never went home. As a child she had loved the piano and organ, but because of inadequate or brutal teachers, she too had given up music. Now, she became fascinated by the early music I was steeping myself in. After we re-collected the harpsichord, we also got her the clavichord, the spinet, then a small Celtic harp. She plays on Sunday mornings at a nearby Catholic church and though, being allergic to churches, I do not go to listen, I hear her practicing all the time at home. When downstairs, she plays the

Kurzweil; upstairs in her study, she plays the clavichord—whose voice is so soft it's like taking your pulse—you're not sure whether you hear or feel it. Besides, with all the stereo equipment and the myriad early and chamber music discs with which I clutter the house, we are surrounded by music. For many years, we had established a custom or finishing off each work week by driving some sixty miles or so to our music teacher, where Kathy would take a harpsichord lesson then I would take a singing lesson.

Not only does she read music surer and faster than anyone I've known, she also figures our yearly taxes, corrects our diet, and quickly forgets jokes (which can then be retold). Best of all, she sticks around. I feel a little like Odysseus washed up on the island of Drepane, where he discovered Nausicaä who was not only a princess but young, affectionate, and did her own laundry.

How could I be anything but glad that I gave up music? It never gave *me* up, but stayed and controlled my doings as I once imagined only a lifelong love—probably a lost love—could do. My only complaint is that, despite my earlier bravado about Kokoschka's young loves, if I'd known things work out this way, I'd certainly have found more things to give up sooner. On the other hand, I also have sworn, again and again, to give up marrying; fortunately, I've kept that resolution just as poorly. If music has made a more constant mistress than a wife, it's still better to have a wife or mistress who constantly makes music.

ACKNOWLEDGMENTS

Grateful acknowledgment is made to the editors of the following journals where chapters of this book first appeared:

Salmagundi, The Southern Review, The Syracuse Scholar, The Georgia Review, The Paris Review, and *The Yale Review.*

ABOUT THE AUTHOR

Responsible for the emergence of American confessional poetry, W. D. Snodgrass won the 1960 Pulitzer Prize for Poetry for his first book, *Heart's Needle*. He saw much of our domestic suffering as occurring against a backdrop of a more universal suffering inherent in the whole of human experience. Snodgrass followed that astonishing work with *After Experience*; *The Führer Bunker: A Cycle of Poems in Progress* (BOA Editions, Ltd., 1977), nominated for the National Book Critics Circle Award for Poetry and produced by Wynn Handman for the American Place Theater; *Each in His Season* (BOA, 1993); *The Fuehrer Bunker: The Complete Cycle* (BOA, 1995); and *Selected Translations* (BOA, 1998). He is the subject of two recent critical studies, *W. D. Snodgrass in Conversation with Philip Hoy* (Between the Lines, UK), and *Tuned and Under Tension: The Recent Poetry of W. D. Snodgrass*, by Philip Raisor (Univ. of Delaware). He lives with his wife, critic and translator Kathleen Snodgrass, in Erieville, New York, and San Miguel de Allende, Mexico.

BOA EDITIONS, LTD.
AMERICAN READER SERIES